Cambridgeshire
and the Fens

W A L K S

Compiled by
Brian Conduit

Acknowledgements
My thanks for the valuable advice and numerous useful
leaflets that I obtained from Cambridgeshire and
Peterborough councils and the various tourist information
centres throughout the area.

Text:	Brian Conduit
	Revised text for 2006 edition,
	Dennis and Jan Kelsall
Photography:	Brian Conduit
Editorial:	Ark Creative, Norwich
Design:	Ark Creative, Norwich

Series Consultant: Brian Conduit

OS Ordnance Survey® This product includes mapping data licensed
from Ordnance Survey® with the permission
of the Controller of Her Majesty's Stationery Office. © Crown
Copyright 2006. All rights reserved. Licence number 100017593.
Ordnance Survey, the OS symbol and Pathfinder are
registered trademarks and Explorer, Landranger and
Outdoor Leisure are trademarks of the Ordnance Survey,
the national mapping agency of Great Britain.

Jarrold Publishing
ISBN-10: 0-7117-2080-0
ISBN-13: 978-0-7117-2080-0

While every care has been taken to ensure the accuracy of
the route directions, the publishers cannot accept
responsibility for errors or omissions, or for changes in
details given. The countryside is not static: hedges and
fences can be removed, field boundaries can alter, footpaths
can be rerouted and changes in ownership can result in the
closure or diversion of some concessionary paths. Also, paths
that are easy and pleasant for walking in fine conditions may
become slippery, muddy and difficult in wet weather, while
stepping stones across rivers and streams may become
impassable.
    If you find an inaccuracy in either the text or maps, please
write to or e-mail Jarrold Publishing at the addresses below.

First published 2002
by Jarrold Publishing
Revised and reprinted 2006.

Printed in Singapore. 2/06

Jarrold Publishing
Pathfinder Guides, Whitefriars, Norwich NR3 1JR
email: info@totalwalking.co.uk
www.totalwalking.co.uk

Front cover: Buckden Towers
Previous page: Quy Water

Contents

The National Trust; The Ramblers'
Association; Walkers and the Law;
Countryside Access Charter; Walking
Safety; Useful Organisations;
Ordnance Survey Maps

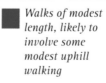

■ Short, easy walks

■ Walks of modest
length, likely to
involve some
modest uphill
walking

■ More challenging
walks which may
be longer and/or
over more rugged
terrain, often with
some stiff climbs

PETERBOROUGH
WHITTLESEY
OUNDLE
RAMSEY
WARBOYS
HUNTINGDON
GODMANCHESTER
ST NEOTS
BEDFORD
KEMPSTON
SANDY
BIGGLESWADE

SCALE 1:277 777 or 1 INCH to about 4½ MILES 1CM to 2.7KM

KILOMETRES

MILES

KEYMAP HEIGHTS SHOWN IN FEET

Major towns and features shown on the map:

MARCH · CHATTERIS · ELY · DOWNHAM MARKET · NEWMARKET · CAMBRIDGE · Littleport · Soham · Isleham · Fordham · Burwell · Waterbeach · Histon · Girton · Cottenham · Willingham · Longstanton · Chesterton · Trumpington · Great Shelford · Little Shelford · Sawston · Linton · Haddenham · Stretham · Sutton · Mepal · Wimblington · Manea · Welney · Outwell · Upwell · Christchurch · Denver · Hilgay · Southery · Methwold Fens · West Dereham · Bexwell · Wimbotsham · Moulton · Cheveley · Dullingham · Fulbourn · Bottisham · Swaffham Prior · Swaffham Bulbeck · Wicken · Reach · Exning · Newmarket Heath

Roads: A47 · A141 · A142 · A14 · A10 · A11 · A1101 · A1122 · A1123 · A1303 · A1307 · A134 · M11 · B1040 · B1049 · B1050 · B1093 · B1098 · B1099 · B1100 · B1101 · B1102 · B1103 · B1104 · B1382 · B1411

Numbered tour markers: 1 · 3 · 7 · 8 · 10 · 11 · 15 · 17 · 18 · 19 · 20 · 22 · 24 · 27

BEDFORD LEVEL · SOUTH LEVEL · The Hundred Foot Washes · Old Bedford River · New Bedford River · R. Great Ouse · River Lark · Little Ouse River · River Cam · River Nene · Ten Mile Bank · Sixteen Foot Drain

At-a-glance...

Walk	Page	Start	Nat. Grid Reference	Distance	Time
Barnack, Helpston and Ufford	76	Barnack	TL 079050	7$\frac{1}{2}$ miles (12.1km)	4 hrs
Buckden and Offord Cluny	30	Buckden	TL 192676	5$\frac{1}{2}$ miles (8.9km)	2$\frac{1}{2}$ hrs
Castor Hanglands	70	Castor	TL 124984	7 miles (11.3km)	3$\frac{1}{2}$ hrs
Elton	18	Elton	TL 089935	4$\frac{1}{4}$ miles (6.8km)	2 hrs
Ely and Little Downham	83	Ely, Tourist Information Centre	TL 537802	10$\frac{1}{2}$ miles (16.9km)	5$\frac{1}{2}$ hrs
Ely and Little Thetford	58	Ely, Tourist Information Centre	TL 537802	7 miles (11.3km)	3$\frac{1}{2}$ hrs
Ferry Meadows, River Nene and Peterborough	80	Ferry Meadows Country Park	TL 148974	10$\frac{1}{4}$ miles (16.5km)	5$\frac{1}{4}$ hrs
Gog Magog Hills and the Granta Valley	73	Wandlebury Country Park	TL 492532	7 miles (11.3km)	3$\frac{1}{2}$ hrs
Grafham Water	87	Grafham Water Visitor Centre	TL 166681	9$\frac{1}{4}$ miles (14.9km)	5 hrs
Grantchester Meadows and Cambridge	27	Grantchester	TL 433554	6 miles (9.7km)	3 hrs
Isleham	53	Isleham	TL 643744	6$\frac{1}{2}$ miles (10.5km)	3 hrs
Kimbolton	14	Kimbolton	TL 100677	3$\frac{1}{2}$ miles (5.6km)	1$\frac{1}{2}$ hrs
Linton, Hildersham and the Roman Road	67	Linton	TL 561468	7 miles (11.3km)	3$\frac{3}{4}$ hrs
Lolworth, Knapwell and Boxworth	47	Lolworth	TL 366641	6 miles (9.7km)	3hrs
Mepal and the Hundred Foot Drain	12	Mepal	TL 439814	3 miles (4.8km)	1$\frac{1}{2}$ hrs
Over and Swavesey	16	Over	TL 373707	4$\frac{3}{4}$ miles (7.6km)	2$\frac{1}{2}$ hrs
Ramsey and Bury	22	Ramsey, Abbey Green	TL 290851	5 miles (8km)	2$\frac{1}{2}$ hrs
Reach, Swaffham Prior and the Devil's Dyke	24	Reach	TL 567660	4$\frac{1}{2}$ miles (7.2km)	2$\frac{1}{2}$ hrs
St Ives, Houghton and the Hemingfords	38	St Ives	TL 314713	6 miles (9.7km)	3hrs
St Neots and Little Paxton	50	St Neots, Riverside Park	TL 180601	7$\frac{1}{4}$ miles (11.7km)	3$\frac{1}{2}$ hrs
Sawtry and the Giddings	64	Sawtry, St Judith's Lane car park	TL 172831	7$\frac{1}{2}$ miles (12.1km)	3$\frac{1}{2}$ hrs
Stilton and Folksworth	44	Stilton	TL 163894	6 miles (9.7km)	3hrs
Stow cum Quy Fen	33	Lode	TL 534626	5$\frac{1}{2}$ miles (8.9km)	2$\frac{1}{2}$ hrs
Wansford, Sutton, Upton and Thornhaugh	41	Wansford	TL 075991	8 miles (12.9km)	4$\frac{1}{2}$ hrs
Wicken Fen	36	Wicken Fen, Nat. Trust car park	TL 565706	6 miles (9.7km)	3 hrs
Willingham and the Great Ouse	56	Willingham	TL 404705	6$\frac{1}{2}$ miles (10.5km)	3 hrs
Wimblington and Stonea Camp	61	Wimblington	TL 415921	7$\frac{1}{2}$ miles (12.1km)	3$\frac{1}{2}$ hrs
Wimpole Park	20	Wimpole Hall	TL 338509	5 miles (8km)	2$\frac{1}{2}$ hrs

Comments

Three delightful limestone villages, all with fine medieval churches, are linked by tracks and field and woodland paths.

Buckden has a fine church and the remains of a bishops' palace, and there are extensive views across the valley of the Great Ouse on the walk to Offord Cluny.

The walk takes you through the lovely woodlands and across the open heathland of Castor Hanglands to the north of the River Nene.

This is an easy walk in the pleasant countryside of the Nene Valley, with the chance to visit a late-medieval manor house.

The towers of Ely Cathedral are seen from many different angles on this splendid and lengthy walk, mainly along drove roads, across the Isle of Ely.

The outward stretch is mainly across fields, the return leg is beside the Great Ouse, with almost constant views of Ely Cathedral.

The route combines a circuit of Ferry Meadow Country Park with a walk along the banks of the River Nene. The longer walk includes the centre of Peterborough and the cathedral.

From an Iron Age fort on the Gog Magog Hills, the route descends into the Granta Valley. A walk through the valley is followed by an easy climb onto a ridge for a superb climax along a tree-lined Roman road.

This extended circuit of the reservoir includes two villages, varied walking and fine view across the water.

A popular walk with residents, this is a great way to reach the heart of Cambridge and explore its wealth of fascinating buildings.

This flat Fenland walk to the south and west of Isleham uses tracks, field paths and part of a disused railway line.

The walk takes you onto the low hills to the north of Kimbolton and there are fine views over the village on the descent.

After climbing a ridge, the route continues along a stretch of Roman road before descending into Hildersham and through the Granta Valley.

This walk, mainly along broad tracks, is in the gently undulating countryside to the south of the Great Ouse and links three quiet villages.

The first and last parts of this short and easy walk are beside the Hundred Foot Drain, dug as part of the 17th-century drainage of the Fens.

Two Fenland villages in the valley of the Great Ouse are linked by tracks, field paths and embankments. There are wide views across the Fens.

The walk starts in the historic village of Ramsey, with its monastic remains, and there are wide views across the Fens.

This route includes two attractive Fenland villages and ends with a walk along the Devil's Dyke, a Dark Age defence and fine viewpoint.

A perfect riverside walk, which starts in a historic town and includes three picturesque villages, medieval churches, thatched cottage, old mill and beautiful meadows.

A relaxing walk from the town through old meadows by the River Great Ouse to a nearby nature reserve that has been created from abandoned sand and gravel workings.

The walk is across gently undulating country to the south-west of Peterborough, visiting two small hamlets, one of which has great historical interest.

From the village of Stilton, the route takes you across undulating country, passing the site of a deserted village and the earthworks of a motte-and-bailey castle.

An attractive walk across open fenland is enhanced by a pretty village, old mill, tree-lined channel and the chance to visit a restored 17th-century house.

This route to the west of Peterborough takes in four attractive villages and includes some splendid walking beside the River Nene.

This walk takes you around the edge of the National Trust's Wicken Fen nature reserve, one of the few remaining areas of undrained fenland.

Wide and straight tracks link Willingham with the Great Ouse, and the middle stretch of the walk is along an embankment above the river.

This Fenland walk of wide and extensive views take you from the village of Wimblington to the earth-works of a Roman fort.

A large and imposing country house and fine views across the extensive parkland are the chief attractions of this walk.

At-a-glance...

Introduction to Cambridgeshire and the Fens

Statistically, Cambridgeshire is the flattest county in England. Although its highest point – at Great Chishill in the south of the county, near the Hertfordshire and Essex borders – rises to 480ft (146m), this is exceptional, and the average height is considerably lower. On an Ordnance Survey map of the Fens, contour lines are virtually non-existent. The Fens cover a considerable part of Cambridgeshire and feature prominently in this walking guide, but there is more to the county than their flat expanses. Gently undulating country and some hills, albeit fairly low ones, are to be found in the west and south.

Riverside scenery and historic landscapes

Despite what enthusiastic hill-walkers often say, flat terrain is neither boring nor featureless, and Cambridgeshire has much to offer walkers. This includes some lovely riverside scenery, fine old towns, attractive villages and much of historic interest, all set within a pleasant and gentle landscape. The Fens themselves are of great interest to those keen on landscape history and development, and their immense flatness does have a uniquely fascinating quality that is difficult to define, perhaps possessing something of the attraction of the desert wastes of the Sahara or the polar wastes of the Arctic. Much of the walking in the Fens is along straight, broad drove roads or on the top of embankments above the rivers and drainage channels, from which you can fully enjoy the wide and expansive views.

Attractive villages

Cambridgeshire was one of the counties that was enlarged as a result of the boundary changes of 1974. The north-west used to be in Northamptonshire – the historic Soke of Peterborough. This is limestone country, part of the belt of oolitic limestone that runs in a north-easterly direction from the Cotswolds to Yorkshire. This gently undulating landscape, watered by the beautiful River Nene, contains villages which, though less commercialised, are just as attractive as many of their better-known Cotswold counterparts.

Fine old market towns, water and chalk hills

The west is the former small county of Huntingdonshire, also absorbed into Cambridgeshire in 1974. This contains a slice of Fenland but also much undulating country. The area is noted for the string of fine old market towns and picturesque villages located near the banks of the Great Ouse. A more recent feature of the landscape is Grafham Water, a large reservoir created in the 1960s. It has now become an important wildlife and recreational area, particularly valuable in a county lacking in natural lakes. Almost as valuable an asset are the cluster of lakes in the valley of the Great Ouse around St Ives, Huntingdon and St Neots, created from the extraction of sand and gravel.

Approaching Elton church

The hilliest country in Cambridgeshire is to be found in the south, near the Essex and Hertford-shire borders. Here there is a series of chalk outcrops, forming part of the chalk range which extends across eastern England from the Chilterns. One of these outcrops is the Gog Magog Hills, topped by the Iron Age hillfort of Wandlebury Ring, now the focal point of a popular country park within easy reach of Cambridge.

The Fens

The Fens are undoubtedly the dominant feature of the Cambridgeshire landscape, extending over much of the central, eastern and northern parts of the county and spreading over the borders into neighbouring west Norfolk and south Lincolnshire. Centuries ago the whole area was a vast expanse of water and marsh, inhabited by people who lived on the drier 'islands' which rose above the waterlogged lowlands, eking out a living from fish, eels and wildfowl. It was on these marshlands – difficult to penetrate without knowledge of the terrain – that the semi-legendary Saxon hero Hereward the Wake held out against the Norman conquerors for many years after 1066.

From the earliest days man tried to use the Fens, and a process of gradual reclamation of the land for farming took place. In the Middle Ages this was spearheaded by the many great monasteries in the area but it was not until the 17th century that the drainage of the Fens began on a large and systematic scale. The men mainly responsible for initiating this were the fourth Duke of Bedford and the Dutch engineer Cornelius Vermuyden. Vermuyden's major project involved the digging of two parallel channels about 21 miles (34km) long between Earith and Denver – the Old and New Bedford rivers – leaving an area in between (the Ouse Washes) that could absorb flooding in the winter and be used as pasture in the summer. This and other schemes were bitterly opposed by local people because it threatened their traditional fishing and wildfowling rights, but the schemes went ahead and by the 19th century most of the Fens had been drained and converted into what is now an intensive and highly productive area of vegetable, flower and fruit growing.

There are few places left where you can see some of the original undrained Fenland but one is Wicken Fen, roughly halfway between Cambridge and Ely. This is Britain's oldest nature reserve and is maintained by the National Trust.

Cambridge and Grantchester

The Great Ouse is the county's principal river and Cambridge, one of England's finest and most distinctive historic cities, is situated on the banks of one of its tributaries, the Cam. The Norman conquerors built a castle here in the late 11th century, the first scholars arrived in 1209 and the first college (Peterhouse) was founded in 1284. It is the combination of river and college buildings that gives Cambridge its unique charm. As the Cam meanders along the 'backs' of the colleges, it makes a delightful scene, flowing between willow-lined banks, under a variety of bridges, with people punting or rowing, especially on languid summer afternoons. Finest view of all from the river is probably that of King's College Chapel, a building of perfect proportions and quite breathtaking beauty.

A short distance upstream from Cambridge is the idyllic village of Grantchester, easily reached by boat or across Grantchester Meadows by bicycle or on foot. Rupert Brooke lived here before the outbreak of the First World War and immortalised the village in his nostalgic poem *The Old Vicarage, Grantchester*. After the war it became a major artistic and intellectual centre, and something of the flavour and atmosphere of those days can still be sampled by sitting under the trees in the garden of the Orchard Tea Rooms, a traditional haunt of many visitors to Grantchester.

Ely, Peterborough, stately homes, Stonea and Devil's Dyke

Apart from the Cambridge colleges, the foremost historic attractions of Cambridgeshire are the great Norman cathedrals of Ely and Peterborough. In particular Ely, situated on one of the Fenland 'islands', ranks as one of the outstanding cathedrals of Europe and appears almost to float above the surrounding flat terrain. There are smaller monastic remains at Thorney, Ramsey, Denny and Isleham, and the county's fine stately homes include Wimpole Hall, Anglesey Abbey, Elton Hall and Hinchingbrooke House. Wimpole Hall is probably the most imposing of these, set in lovely rolling parkland near the Hertfordshire border.

Other historic attractions include the Roman fort at Stonea Camp near March, the old bridge over the Great Ouse at St Ives, with its rare medieval chapel – one of only four in England – and a number of outstanding parish

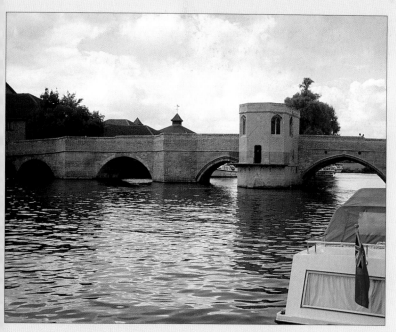

The medieval bridge and chapel at St Ives

churches. Two historic features provide some superb walking: the Roman road that runs along the chalk ridge and the Devil's Dyke, an impressive Dark Age earthwork.

Walking in the area

There are a number of long-distance routes in Cambridgeshire – Fen Rivers Way, Nene Way, Ouse Valley Way, Icknield Way, Hereward Way and so on – which provide pleasant, easy-to-follow and satisfying walking, and most paths are well-waymarked.

Obviously in a walking guide to an area like this, there are no really difficult or challenging routes so the orange-coded walks are placed in that category purely because of their length. The greatest difficulties a walker is likely to encounter are muddy conditions after rain or during winter months and overgrown paths and tracks in the middle of summer, especially on those tracks tightly enclosed by trees and hedges. This is a small price to pay for the enjoyment of a combination of gently undulating slopes, wide and open expanses, huge skies, lazily winding rivers, appealing old towns and attractive villages, which are all ingredients of the Cambridgeshire landscape.

A final point is that, during the winter, some of the riverside meadows, especially those beside the Great Ouse, are regularly flooded. This is likely to affect parts of Walks 12, 16 and possibly others. If this occurs, you can complete the walks by using the adjacent roads.

Mepal and the Hundred Foot Drain

Start	Mepal, parking spaces where road ends on west side of Mepal Bridge
Distance	3 miles (4.8km)
Approximate time	1½ hours
Parking	By Mepal Bridge
Refreshments	Pub by Mepal Bridge
Ordnance Survey maps	Landranger 143 (Ely & Wisbech), Explorer 228 (March & Ely)

This short walk starts and finishes with pleasant riverside stretches beside the New Bedford River or Hundred Foot Drain, overlooking the Ouse Washes. In between, the route takes you mainly along enclosed tracks and paths that encircle the Fenland village of Mepal. Some of these may be muddy after rain and become overgrown during the summer.

Begin by crossing the bridge and turn left along a track to a gate. Go through and walk along the top of the embankment above the Hundred Foot Drain or New Bedford River. This and the parallel Old Bedford River are two huge channels dug in the 17th century as part of the draining of the Fens. They

The Hundred Foot Drain at Mepal

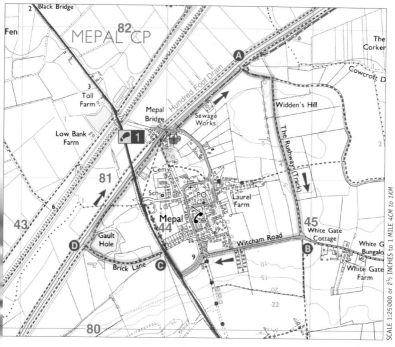

SCALE 1:25 000 or 2½ INCHES to 1 MILE 4CM to 1KM

both run in almost a straight line for over 20 miles (32km) and link up with the Great Ouse at both ends. The area in between, the washes, is really an overflow channel to contain winter flooding.

Look out for where you turn right over a stile, turn left along the parallel track below the embankment and, immediately after crossing a brick bridge, turn right along a track **A**.

After about 200 yds (183m), follow the main track to the right, cross a drain and walk along the left-hand edge of fields. The route then continues – first along a narrow enclosed path and later along a hedge-lined track – to a road **B**.

Turn right to a T-junction, turn left to the A142, turn right and, after 200 yds (183m), turn left, at a public footpath sign, along an enclosed path **C**.

Climb a stile to emerge from the trees and continue along an embankment to another stile. To the right are the wetlands and pool of the Gault Nature Reserve, created through the digging of clay. After climbing the stile, turn right **D** to descend the embankment; climb another stile and keep ahead through bushes to continue along a riverside path again.

The route continues by the Hundred Foot Drain, passing through small belts of trees and bushes and going through several kissing-gates. It also passes under the A142. *If the footpath under the bridge is flooded – as sometimes happens in winter – an alternative is to cross the road using stiles.* After the bridge, continue along the right-hand edge of a meadow and go through a kissing-gate onto a tarmac path. At this point it is worth a short detour to the right to see Mepal's small 13th-century church, heavily restored by the Victorians. The route continues to the left, passing beside the Three Pickerels pub to a road. Turn left over the bridge to return to the start. ●

Kimbolton

Start	Kimbolton
Distance	3½ miles (5.6km)
Approximate time	1½ hours
Parking	Kimbolton, parking spaces in High Street
Refreshments	Pubs at Kimbolton
Ordnance Survey maps	Landranger 153 (Bedford & Huntingdon, St Neots & Biggleswade), Explorer 225 (Huntingdon & St Ives)

The walk takes you up onto the open and gentle slopes of Warren Hill, which rises to a height of 232ft (71m) to the north of Kimbolton. The views are fine and extensive, especially on the descent, where the town, church and imposing mansion of Kimbolton Castle are spread out below you.

The small town of Kimbolton has the medieval church at one end of the High Street and the 18th-century castle at the other. The church dates mainly from the 13th century; the tower and spire were added in the 14th century and the south porch in the 15th. Kimbolton Castle was rebuilt in the early 18th century by Vanbrugh as an elegant country house

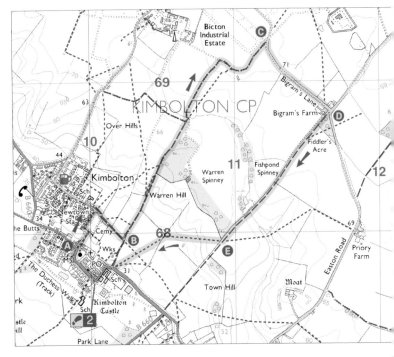

Kimbolton

for the first Duke of Manchester and was added to, later in the century, by Robert Adam. It is now a school.

🖊 Start at the bottom end of High Street at the corner of Castle Green and, with your back to the castle, walk along High Street towards the church. The road curves right by the church and, where it bends left, keep ahead Ⓐ along a narrow lane (Carnaby). Continue along a tarmac path, bear left on joining another path and cross a footbridge over the little River Kym. Turn left in front of cemetery gates. The path then turns right to continue alongside the cemetery wall to a T-junction.

Turn left, immediately turn right, at a public footpath sign, to enter a field and turn right along its right-hand edge, passing the backs of cottages. Bear slightly right to continue along a broad, hedge-lined track to a T-junction and turn left Ⓑ onto another hedge-lined track which heads gently uphill and continues along the left-hand edge of a field. In the field corner, turn left through a hedge gap and turn right to continue along the right-hand edge of a field, by Warren Spinney on the right. Head over the brow of Warren Hill and,

after passing a Huntingdonshire Country Walks sign, keep ahead to join a concrete track and follow it around a left-hand bend. The area around here is a disused airfield. Turn right onto another concrete track to a T-junction: turn right and the track curves left to emerge onto a lane Ⓒ.

Turn right and, at a T-junction, turn right at a public bridleway sign onto a track Ⓓ which passes to the left of farm buildings. At a fork, take the left-hand, enclosed track, by woodland on the left, to enter a field. The route now continues in a straight line along the right-hand edge of a succession of fields. After passing along the left-hand edge of Warren Spinney, look out for a hedge gap and turn right through it Ⓔ.

Follow a clear path diagonally downhill across a field. From here there is a superb view of Kimbolton Castle, village and church spire.

On the far side of the field, bear slightly left to continue diagonally across the next field and, in the far corner, keep ahead to a track. Turn left, recross the River Kym to reach a road and turn right. Follow the road around first a left-hand and then a right-hand bend to return to the starting point on High Street. ●

Over and Swavesey

Start	Over
Distance	4¾ miles (7.6km)
Approximate time	2½ hours
Parking	Small car park beside church
Refreshments	The White Horse at Swavesey
Ordnance Survey maps	Landranger 154 (Cambridge & Newmarket), Explorer 225 (Huntingdon & St Ives)

This undemanding walk straddles the Greenwich Meridian and follows Swavesey Drain to the River Great Ouse. After striking across fields to Swavesey, where there is a convenient pub, it returns past old orchards. The churches of both villages hold interest and there are pleasing views from the relative heights of the embankments that contain the watercourses.

Medieval Over was one of the largest settlements in the area and, like its neighbour Swavesey, was dependent for transport and communication on the Great Ouse. Locally grown woad was used to produce a blue dye, an industry that brought relative prosperity to the village. This wealth is reflected in the development of its church, originally Saxon, but rebuilt with stone brought across the marshes from Barnack, almost 30 miles (48km) away. An unusual feature is the stone bench around the walls, seating for the elderly at a time when the congregation was expected to stand or kneel throughout the service.

Leaving the small parking area, follow the lane past the church. After some ¼ mile (400m), turn off into Lowburyholme Road **A**, signed as a footpath to Overcote. Degrading to a track, the way continues between outgrown hedges. Swing left in front of the entrance to a field and later cross a stile before climbing onto a flood embankment. To the right, a path follows the crest above Swavesey Drain, dug to take barges from the river to a wharf at Swavesey.

Reaching Webbs Hole Sluice **B**, turn across the bridge and walk forward on another embankment that soon curves parallel with the river. Pleasure boats pass to and fro and, across the low-lying fields to the left, a tapering spire and square tower mark the churches of Over and Swavesey respectively. Follow the raised path, crossing occasional stiles for just over ½ mile (800m) to reach a gate across the dike **C**. Drop left onto a tall-hedged track, which strikes a straight line dividing the fields. At its end, turn right onto another track. Later curving, it crosses a disused railway line before finally finishing at the edge of Swavesey **D**.

The church lies a short distance to the left, set back from the road behind its extensive graveyard. It stands on the site of an early priory, established before the Normans arrived on these shores. Inside, the ends of each pew are decorated with a carved head, some dating from the

15th century whilst others are Victorian copies of the originals.

The onward route, however, lies to the right, winding through the village to a junction beside the White Horse **E**. Turn beside it into Market Street, walking on the right-hand side to continue past the village green. Degrading to a track, the way soon forks and you should take the left branch signed to Over. Breaks in the hedge allow a view back to the church, in front of which is the part-timbered building of Manor Farm. Carry on, re-crossing the old railway line and later a drain, where to the right, a windmill can be seen in the middle distance – one of many that once dotted the fens. Keep on past a succession of fruit orchards, at the far side of which, a farm track leads out to a lane **F**.

Cross diagonally right to an enclosed footpath that winds into a small housing estate. Emerging onto a street,

Swavesey

follow it ahead and then left. After passing Denny Close, turn off left along a pleasant tree-lined grass track that skirts the houses. Meeting another street at the far end, swing right back onto the estate and then go left, walking out to the main lane. Retrace your outward steps right back to the church. ●

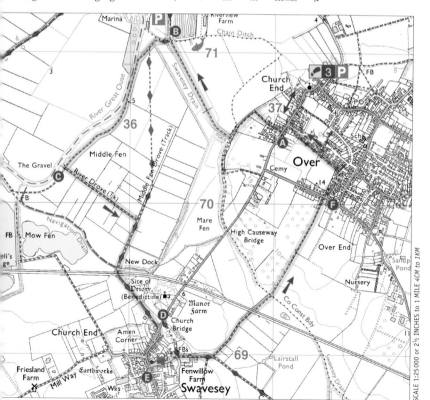

Elton

Start	All Saints' Church, Elton
Distance	4¼ miles (6.8km)
Approximate time	2 hours
Parking	Roadside parking at Elton
Refreshments	Pub at Elton and café at Elton Hall garden centre
Ordnance Survey maps	Landranger 142 (Peterborough), Explorer 227 (Peterborough)

This uncomplicated walk straddles the Cambridgeshire – Northamptonshire border, exploring the pleasant Nene Valley countryside south of the village of Elton. There are glimpses during the latter stage across the park to Elton Hall. Home of the Proby family since 1660, it is open to the public and stands amidst exquisite gardens.

Elton Hall (tel. 01832 280468) stands on the site of a Norman manor and was begun by Sir Peter Proby, Lord Mayor of London and Comptroller of the Royal Household after being granted the estate by Elizabeth I. The superb decorations, furnishings and art treasures reflect the changing styles during its 350 years as a family home, an evolution most recently expressed in the Gothic orangery and garden created to celebrate the millennium.

Head from the church away from the village along the B671, later passing the entrance to Elton Hall. Reaching the busy main road, carefully cross and go left to turn up a private lane onto the Elton Estate Ⓐ. Abandon it just a short distance along through a waymarked gate on the right and strike across the field to another gate by the corner of a wood. Keep ahead at the perimeter of the next field, joining a track at its far side that runs ahead beside Blue Bell Spinney.

Reaching the end of the wood, the track swings right and left along the field edge. A copse at the far side is side-stepped to the left before crossing a plank bridge through a gap in the hedge to gain the next field. Keep with the right-hand boundary to resume your southerly heading, soon arriving at a T-junction Ⓑ.

To the right, the track runs between open fields for over ¹/₂ mile (800m), eventually ending at a lane. Go left, later bending with it in front of a

Elton church

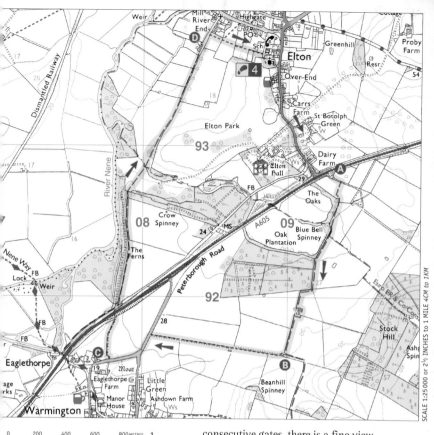

0	200	400	600	800 METRES	1
					KILOMETRES
					MILES

0	200	400	600 YARDS	½

junction. Then, just after passing Dexter Way, turn off through a waymarked gate on the right **C**. Walk forward, mounting a stile to carry on at the field edge. Where it subsequently curves above a cutting, look for a kissing-gate from which a contained path drops back to the main road. Carefully cross to the continuation of the path opposite that leads through to a track.

Turn right and climb past a turning area to a bridleway signed off left through a gate. It rises below a communications transmitter to continue outside the field edge. Later slipping into the bordering woodland, maintain your forward direction above the Nene, which although close by is hardly visible through the trees. However, passing out through consecutive gates, there is a fine view across the park to Elton Hall. Bearing slightly right, head down to a bridge beside a gate.

The onward track rises around the edge of thicket before running above a succession of large fields. Developing into a lane as it passes cottages, keep on a little farther to reach more houses on the right **D**. Turn off over a stile beside a gate on the right immediately before them and strike out across the meadows towards Elton church. Leave over a stile by a gate at the top, just left of the church and go right behind the village school into the churchyard. Below the northwest corner of the tower are two Saxon wheel-headed gravemarkers, however, little else of its early fabric remains, as it was largely rebuilt in the 15th century and subsequently twice restored. Walk out through the churchyard to return to the start. ●

Wimpole Park

Start	Wimpole Hall
Distance	5 miles (8km)
Approximate time	2½ hours
Parking	Car park at Wimpole Hall (National Trust)
Refreshments	Restaurant and café at Wimpole Hall
Ordnance Survey maps	Landranger 154 (Cambridge & Newmarket), Explorers 209 (Cambridge) and 208 (Bedford & St Neots)

Wimpole lies amidst the folds of the gentle hills that rise to the west of Cambridge, and this ramble around the park and neighbouring farmland exploits the views to the full. The 17th-century hall looks out over 60 acres (24.3 hectares) of formal garden, both well worth visiting at the end of the walk.

Begun in 1640, Wimpole Hall (National Trust, tel. 01223 206000) has been extended and remodelled over the centuries and has become Cambridgeshire's grandest country house. Much of its splendour is due to its last owner, Elsie Bainbridge, daughter of Rudyard Kipling, who restored the house after her husband's death and refurnished the main rooms. The park and gardens are no less impressive, and include the work of several noted gardeners including 'Capability' Brown and Humphry Repton.

From the car park, walk around to the stable block entrance below the clock tower and go through a metal gate directly opposite, from which a path is signed to the hall and gardens. It leads past the church, rebuilt by the Yorkes around 1749 and containing many funerary memorials in the large family chapel, the only remaining part of the original building. Keep ahead, passing between the house and an imposing avenue that runs due south for almost 2½ miles (4km). Carry on to a second gate leading out to the park. Follow the fence right to a ha ha **Ⓐ**, there going left to climb away between young lime trees along West Avenue.

Turning right through a kissing-gate at the top, follow a line of trees away at the edge of a wood. Where the avenue finishes, look for a stile beside a gate into the wood from which a path leads to the right. After some 350 yds (320m), look for a narrower path off right. The short detour takes you back out to the park at the edge of a small lake, across which there is a view to a hilltop folly, the Wimpole Ruins.

Return to the main path and follow it on through the trees until you eventually reach a waymarked junction **Ⓑ**, just before a gate at the edge of the wood. Turn right along a broad track that runs the length of a narrow woodland strip. Emerging onto a lane, go left, climbing a short distance to a sharp bend **Ⓒ**. Waymarked as a bridleway, a track leaves into more woodland on the right. Soon breaking out into more open ground, it continues at the edge of fields, finally leading to a junction beside a

Wimpole Hall

couple of concrete reservoirs 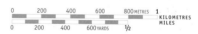.

Turn through a gap in the trees on the right, from which a path, signed to Wimpole, follows the field edge. Approaching the end of the hedge, a waymark directs you through it along an enclosed path. Emerging onto a field track, keep with it down the rolling hillside to Cobb's Wood Farm. Continue past the buildings and over a small bridge, forking right to pass in front of a lodge. Meeting a lane at the end, go left and then turn in at the visitor entrance to Wimpole Hall to return to the car park. ●

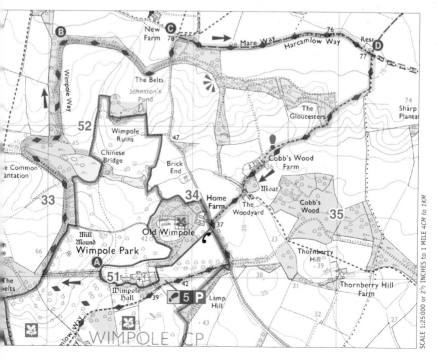

SCALE 1:25 000 or 2½ INCHES to 1 MILE 4CM to 1KM

Ramsey and Bury

Start	Ramsey, Abbey Green
Distance	5 miles (8km)
Approximate time	2½ hours
Parking	Ramsey, parking spaces by Abbey Green
Refreshments	Pubs and cafés at Ramsey, pub at Bury
Ordnance Survey maps	Landranger 142 (Peterborough), Explorer 227 (Peterborough)

The first part of the walk is across Bury Fen between Ramsey and the adjoining village of Bury. The return leg takes you across part of the disused Upwood Airfield. There is plenty of interest at Ramsey, with its attractive greens, monastic remains and Norman church, and a medieval church at Bury. There are also wide views over the surrounding fens.

The most striking features of Ramsey are the two large greens: Abbey Green and Church Green. The former is bounded by the church and abbey gate-house and the latter, which has a duck pond, by the church and attractive old houses and cottages. Ramsey Abbey, originally founded in 969, was one of the foremost Fenland monasteries but now all that remains is the 15th-century gatehouse and parts of the lady chapel, which have been incorporated into school buildings. The 12th-century church, a fine example of Norman architecture, was originally built as the 'hospitium', a guest house or possibly a hospital, for the monastery, and became a parish church in the 13th century.

🖉 Facing the abbey gatehouse, turn left alongside Church Green, passing to the left of the church. Follow the road as it bends left by the pond. At a public footpath sign – and

a sign to the Rural Museum – turn right along a track **A**.

Go through a kissing-gate. In front of the museum gates, turn left along the right-hand edge of a field. At a hedge corner, turn right to continue by the right-hand field edge. Turn left in the field corner and turn right at a way-marked post. Walk along the right-hand edge of a field to a T-junction; turn right, then right again, along the right-hand edge of the next field. In the corner, follow the field edge to the left and

Church Green, Ramsey

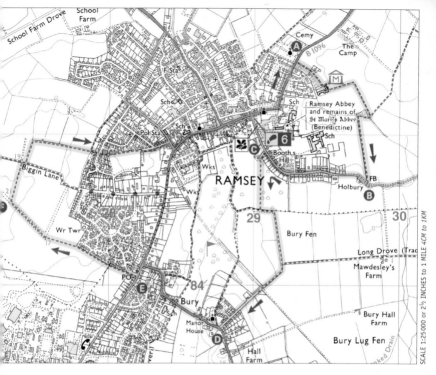

SCALE 1:25000 or 2½ INCHES to 1 MILE 4CM to 1KM

```
0    200   400   600   800 METRES   1
                                    KILOMETRES
                                    MILES
0    200   400   600 YARDS   ½
```

continue in a straight line to a road **B**.

Turn right into Ramsey again and, after ½ mile (800m), turn left **C** at a public footpath sign, along a track to a kissing-gate. Go through, head in a straight line across a golf course – to follow the regular Huntingdonshire Country Walk waymarked posts – and, on the far side, go through a hedge gap to a T-junction. Turn left along an enclosed path, which bends right and continues between fields across Bury Fen, bending right again to emerge onto a lane. Keep ahead to a T-junction **D** and turn right, passing to the left of Bury's medieval church.

The road continues into Bury, bending first right and then left to reach a T-junction by the White Lion pub. Turn left along Upwood Road; take the first road on the right **E** (Grenfell Road) and, where it curves right, turn left through a kissing-gate, at a public foot-

path sign. Walk along the right-hand edge of two fields and, at a hedge corner in the second field, keep ahead across the open, empty, Fenland landscape. On reaching a tarmac drive, continue along it across Upwood Airfield and, about 50 yds (46m) before it bends left, turn right **F** – there is no public footpath sign – onto a clear, worn path across a field.

On the far side, turn right along a track and, almost immediately, turn left, at a public footpath sign, along the left-hand edge of a field. In the corner, turn right to continue along the field edge and, in the next corner, cross a foot-bridge and keep ahead along an enclosed path. Cross a road and walk along the enclosed tarmac path opposite, which continues along the left-hand edge of a playing field and in front of houses to emerge, via a gate, onto a road.

Keep ahead to a T-junction and turn right. At the next T-junction, turn left along High Street to return to the starting point.

●

Reach, Swaffham Prior and the Devil's Dyke

Start	Reach
Distance	4½ miles (7.2km) – 2¾ (4.4km) for short walk
Approximate time	2½ hours –1½ hours for short walk
Parking	Car park at the corner of Fair Green, Reach
Refreshments	Pubs at Reach and Swaffham Prior
Ordnance Survey maps	Landranger 154 (Cambridge & Newmarket), Explorer 226 (Ely & Newmarket)

Known variously as the Devil's Dyke or Ditch, this spectacular earthwork is Cambridgeshire's most prominent archaeological feature. The walk begins from its western end at Reach, crossing the fields to Swaffham Prior, unusual for having two churches occupying the same graveyard. The return is along the dike itself, giving fine views across the open landscape.

Reach's charter for a fair was awarded in 1201, and the size of the green, smaller than it once was, still testifies to a former importance. The village later developed as a busy port, with cargo travelling up the River Cam and along Reach Lode.

🖉 From the car park, strike out across Fair Green to join the street leaving left from its far corner. Signed to Upware and the Devil's Dyke Walk, it twists right then left, at which point, go right along a short track marked to Reach Fen. After crossing a bridge Ⓐ, turn left and follow a track towards Spring Hall Farm, bypassing the buildings on their left to reach a lane.

Go left over a bridge Ⓑ, and then immediately turn off right onto a public byway, Barston Drove. A pleasant track, it curves around a low hill, giving a view across the fields to the churches and windmill of Swaffham Prior.

Reaching a lane Ⓒ, you can shorten the walk by turning left, otherwise follow it in the other direction. Keep going through the village, eventually passing the 18th-century Red Lion, the last survivor of Swaffham Prior's several pubs. Just beyond, turn off into the churchyard up a path past the front of the village's twin churches Ⓓ. Built to serve separate parishes, St Mary's is the older of the two, containing Norman stonework and still in use as a place of worship. Windows in the north aisle shine as the war memorial and look optimistically to a world of peace. The two parishes were amalgamated in 1667 and St Cyriac's is now in the care of the Churches Conservation Trust.

Swing left behind them to a stile and follow the onward path, passing a small green and shortly meeting a street. Cross to the continuation opposite, but after a few yards, detour right along a rising grass path. Emerging in a small orchard at the top, bear left past the

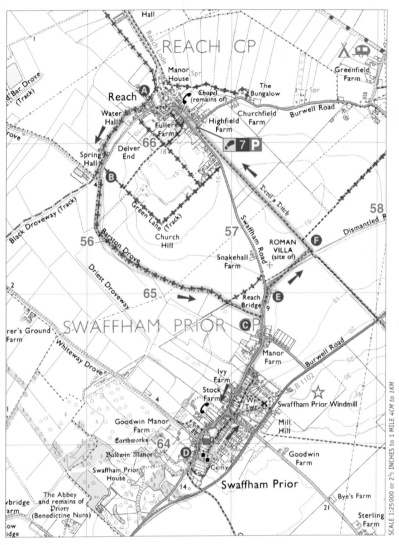

SCALE 1:25000 or 2½ INCHES to 1 MILE 4CM to 1KM

```
0    200    400    600    800 METRES   1
                                        KILOMETRES
                                        MILES
0    200    400    600 YARDS    ½
```

windmill to a drive and turn left back down the hill. Where it bends, keep ahead on a contained path that falls around the perimeter of a garden. Regaining the original path, follow it right, soon winding past sheltered housing to the main village lane.

Turn right, passing the point at which you first joined it **C** to find a concrete track 100 yds (91m) farther along on the right. Immediately beyond it, a narrow path delves into the roadside trees **E**. Bear right to come out at the edge of a field and cut across the corner to a redundant gate. Drop into a disused railway cutting, climbing the opposite embankment a short distance to the right. Follow the field edge right at the top, the Devil's Dyke now a formidable sight in front. The path onto it dips first through its deep, defensive ditch, which is concealed by a clump of trees in the field corner.

Built around the beginning of the 7th century, it served to protect three important routes into East Anglia against raids by British tribes. Running in a straight line for 7½ miles (12km) and, at its highest, 34 feet (10.4m), it remains an impressive statement of Saxon power.

Gaining the top **F**, follow a path left along its crest. There is no obvious trace of the Roman villa that lay across the field to the left, but there is initially a grand panorama over the surrounding countryside. Cambridge lies to the south west whilst in the north west, beyond Wicken Fen, rise the distant towers of Ely's Cathedral. Keep going as the path becomes hedged with bushes, passing through a couple of gates before finally emerging back at Reach onto Fair Green.

●

The village green at Reach

Grantchester Meadows and Cambridge

Start	Grantchester
Distance	6 miles (9.7km)
Approximate time	3 hours
Parking	Street parking in Grantchester
Refreshments	Pubs and tearoom at Grantchester, pubs and cafés in Cambridge
Ordnance Survey maps	Landranger 154 (Cambridge & Newmarket, Saffron Walden), Explorer 209 (Cambridge)

The rivers Cam and Granta combine their waters south of Grantchester, lazily flowing between meadows and lush woodland to the university city of Cambridge. Following its course, this relaxing walk offers a picturesque route to the colleges clustered at the city's ancient heart. Explore at leisure or perhaps take a punt on the river before returning along the bank to the village immortalised in Rupert Brooke's poem.

The son of a Rugby School master, Rupert Brooke attended King's College and settled in Grantchester in 1909, where he began writing poetry. Before the outbreak of war, he travelled widely and wrote *The Old Vicarage, Grantchester* in Berlin during 1912. But it was his war poems that brought him recognition. He enlisted in the Royal Naval Division, but his career came to a premature end with his death in April 1915 whilst en route to the Dardanelles. His body lies on the Greek island of Skyros and there is a memorial to him in the village church here. The Orchard Tea Room retains the quiet charm of that bygone age and its garden is a delightful place to relax over afternoon tea.

Follow the main street through the village north from the church, bearing right at a junction to pass The Robert Brooke pub. Just beyond, leave through a kissing-gate on the right into Grantchester Meadows, the way signed to Cambridge. Strike across on a clear trod, bearing left where it splits and soon joining a tarmac path. To the left, it continues across successive meadows that run down to the river. Eventually becoming enclosed Ⓐ, it leads out to a track that develops into a leafy street.

At a fork before a small garage bear right and at the end of the street, go right again. Follow it left at the bottom, there looking for a kissing-gate on the right. A path delves into the rich woodland of Paradise Nature Reserve, winding beside a stream to join the river. Keep with it beneath pendulous boughs of willows, shortly leaving the main flow beside a leat. Emerging from the wood through a kissing-gate, pass a car park and then swing over a bridge to continue along the channel's opposite bank.

Reaching a main road, cross to resume the waterside path, which soon leads to a millpond overlooked by the former mill. Bear right across the meadows towards the river, following it to a bridge above a weir. Cross and walk out to the street beyond. Go left and then, as the street bends away, keep ahead along a narrow alley, Laundress Lane behind The Anchor pub to emerge on Silver Street **B**.

Turn back over the river and cross the road, swinging right past the corner of Queen's College to join a pleasant path set back from the main road. It leads past the college 'Backs': King's, Clare and Trinity Hall, giving charming views of the buildings. Beyond Trinity Hall, take the pathway on the right,

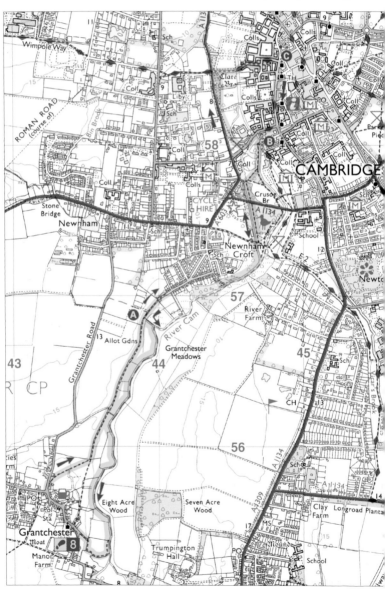

King's College Chapel, Cambridge

Garret Hostel Lane, which leads to a bridge across the river. Carry on between college buildings, turning left and then right into Trinity Lane. Walk up between Trinity and Gonville and Caius Colleges to Trinity Street at the top **C**. You are now in the pedestrianised heart of the city, the various colleges, churches and museums all within easy reach.

Cambridge has been a seat of learning since the beginning of the 13th century, when groups of students moved here from Oxford. Ever since the founding of the first college, Peterhouse in 1284, the university has influenced the character of this lovely city. Magnificent medieval architecture abounds in the college buildings and many churches, the best of all being the chapel of King's College, founded by Henry VI. Begun in 1446, it took almost 100 years to complete, and its exquisitely beautiful fan-vaulted roof portrays Perpendicular architecture at its finest.

The return follows Trinity Street to the right, passing the splendid King's College Chapel. Keep going along King's Parade to a junction overlooked by St Botolph's Church and turn right into Silver Street. Approaching The Anchor, go left back down Laundress Lane to the river, and retrace your steps to the edge of Grantchester Meadows **A**.

Varying the outward route, bear left at the end of the contained track to follow the meandering riverbank. Keep going for some $1\frac{1}{4}$ miles (2km) from meadow to meadow until eventually reaching a stile into a wood. Instead of crossing, follow the field edge away from the river round to a kissing-gate in the top right corner. Walk up to the main lane through the village and turn right back to the church. ●

Buckden and Offord Cluny

Start	Buckden
Distance	5½ miles (8.9km)
Approximate time	2½ hours
Parking	Roadside parking at Buckden
Refreshments	Pubs at Buckden, pub at Offord Cluny
Ordnance Survey maps	Landranger 153 (Bedford & Huntingdon), Explorer 225 (Huntingdon & St Ives)

From Buckden, a gentle descent into the valley of the Great Ouse – across fields, through woodland and by a stream and pools – brings you to the riverside village of Offord Cluny. After a short circuit of the village, the return leg is mostly along a quiet lane. Throughout the walk, there are attractive and expansive views across the valley.

The pale stonework of the impressive 15th-century church and the dark brickwork of the remains of the adjacent Buckden Towers make a striking composition, especially when the sun is shining on them. Buckden Towers was the palace of the medieval bishops of Lincoln and mainly comprises the Great Tower and gate-house, built in the 15th century. Catherine of Aragon, the first of Henry VIII's six wives, lived here in the 1530s, and there is a re-created Tudor walled garden dedicated to her.

Start at the crossroads in the village centre by the Lion and George hotels and walk along Church Street. Just after passing the church, turn right into Manor Gardens. At a fork, take the left-hand road and, at a public footpath sign near where the road ends, turn right to a T-junction in front of a pool. Turn right along a tarmac path, take the left-hand path at a fork and, at the next fork a few yards ahead, take the right-hand path, which bends right over a footbridge and continues to a road.

Turn left, follow the road as it curves right and, at a public footpath sign, turn left up steps and walk along a tarmac path between bungalows. The path turns right, continues alongside garden fences on the right and, where the tarmac ends, you keep along the right-hand edge of a field to a lane **A**.

Cross over the lane and walk along the path opposite, which keeps initially along the right-hand edge of a field and then continues between fields. Over to the left are fine views across the Great Ouse Valley. After crossing a footbridge over Diddington Brook, turn left **B** at a public footpath sign, and keep along the left-hand edge of a succession of fields to emerge onto a tarmac track. Cross the track and then a footbridge, climb a stile and continue through an attractive belt of woodland beside Diddington Brook. The several pools on both sides of the path have been formed from sand and gravel extraction and are a north-

ward extension of those that make up the Paxton Pits Nature Reserve (see Walk 16).

After climbing a stile, continue first along the left-hand edge of a field and later by the right-hand edge of the brook again. In front of a mill building, turn left to cross a footbridge and keep ahead to go through a kissing-gate onto a road **C**. The route continues to the left but it is worthwhile to turn right for a short detour into the village of Offord Cluny.

Cross a series of bridges over various channels of the Great Ouse, passing the buildings of the converted flour mill, and continue over a level-crossing to a T-junction. Turn right through the village and, at a public footpath sign, turn right **D** along an enclosed path to a stile. Climb it and, as you walk across a field, there is a fine view to the right of Offord Cluny church, which dates from the 13th to 15th centuries. The

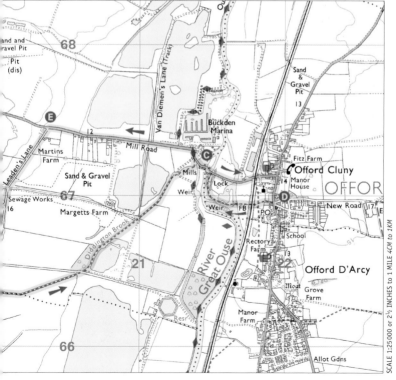

SCALE 1:25 000 or 2½ INCHES to 1 MILE 4CM to 1KM

village is so called because throughout the Middle Ages the French Abbey of Cluny was the lord of the manor.

Climb a stile on the far side of the field and carefully cross the railway line – a traffic lights system operates here as there are four tracks and the trains are fast and frequent. Go through a kissing-gate, keep ahead across a field and then cross three bridges in quick succession over the river. The path continues through trees and curves gradually right to a road. This is where the short circuit around Offord Cluny ends and you turn left for a short stretch to rejoin the previous route.

Cross a bridge, walk past the flour mills again **C** and continue along the road for the next ¾ mile (1.2km), passing Buckden Marina. The village and church spire at Buckden can be seen on the low ridge ahead. Turn left **E** along the lane signposted to Stirtloe, follow it around a right-hand bend and head gently uphill. At a public footpath sign to Buckden, turn right **A** onto a path, here rejoining the outward route, and retrace your steps to the start. ●

Buckden Towers and church

Stow cum Quy Fen

Start	Lode
Distance	5½ miles (8.9km)
Approximate time	2½ hours
Parking	Roadside parking at Lode. When open, the National Trust car park at Anglesey Abbey (tel. 01233 811200) can be used
Refreshments	Café at Anglesey Abbey
Ordnance Survey maps	Landranger 154 (Cambridge & Newmarket), Explorers 209 (Cambridge) and 226 (Ely & Newmarket)

Stow cum Quy Fen – usually shortened to Quy Fen – forms an oasis of pastureland amidst the intensive arable farming country of south Cambridgeshire. It used to be an area of common land between the parishes of Stow cum Quy, Fen Ditton and Horningsea but is now maintained as an open space for local people. The walk follows generally well-defined paths across the fen and passes the picturesque Lode Mill. The views are extensive, and there is a particularly attractive final stretch beside the tree-lined Quy Water. There is also the opportunity to visit Anglesey Abbey, a mainly 17th-century house, and its grounds.

Anglesey Abbey, a Jacobean manor house on the edge of Lode, occupies the site of a medieval priory, and some of the monastic buildings are incorporated into the structure. It had become largely derelict until the estate was bought by Huttleston Broughton, first Lord Fairhaven, in 1926. As well as restoring and extending the house and building up an impressive collection of works of art, he created the superb gardens from previously unpromising fenland.

The walk starts in the High Street at Lode by the post office. At a public footpath sign to Lode Chapel, turn left along a tarmac path which passes to the right of the chapel to a T-junction. Turn right, and almost immediately, turn left to continue first along the right-hand edge of allotments and then along an enclosed path to Lode Mill Ⓐ.

If starting from Anglesey Abbey car park, you walk away from the road along a gravel path and, where it ends, keep ahead to the field edge and turn left. Turn right to continue along the left-hand edge of a field, go through a kissing-gate, walk along an enclosed path and turn left at a hedge corner. In the field corner, turn right; keep along the left-hand edge of fields to a T-junction and turn left along the enclosed path to Lode Mill Ⓐ.

Lode Mill is a working watermill and, like Anglesey Abbey, is owned by the National Trust.

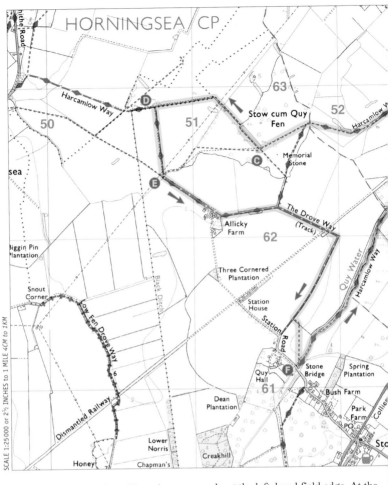

Cross a footbridge over Quy Water, keep ahead along the left-hand edge of a field and, on reaching a belt of woodland, turn right along its right-hand edge to a T-junction. Turn left along a track: at a hedge corner turn right along a hedge-lined track, and, at a T-junction, turn left **B** along another hedge-lined track. On emerging into open country, you reach a three-way fork.

Take the middle route along a path that keeps by the left-hand edge of a field, with a drain running on the left. In the corner, turn right to continue along the left-hand field edge. At the next corner, cross a footbridge over a drain, climb a stile and bear slightly left to a footpath post. The route continues straight ahead along a faint, but discernible, path across rough grass, making for the trees on the far side. Keep along the left-hand edge of the trees to climb a stile and continue along a path that curves right **C** along the left-hand edge of an attractively tree-fringed pool.

At the far end of the pool, turn right over a stile, left along the left-hand edge of a field and, after you cross a footbridge over a drain, the path broadens into a grassy track. The track bends left and continues along the left

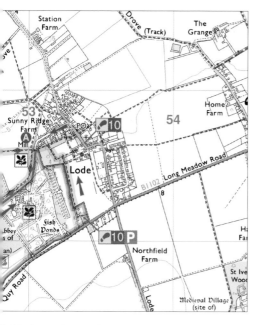

The track later bends right and continues between fields. Look out for a hedge corner on the left, where you go through a kissing-gate and head diagonally across a field to another kissing-gate in the far corner. Do not go through it but turn sharp left **F**, at a public footpath sign to Lode, onto a path beside Quy Water. Now comes a delightful part of the walk as you keep beside the placid and gently winding stream to Lode Mill. Later the banks become tree-lined and there are glimpses of Anglesey Abbey and its grounds on the opposite bank.

field edge as far as a footpath post near a group of trees on the right **D**.

Turn left along the left-hand edge of a field. At a junction of paths and tracks follow the main track, which then curves left **E**, becoming wide and tree-lined.

At Lode Mill **A**, turn right over the bridge to rejoin the outward route and retrace your steps back to the starting point in the High Street. ●

Quy Water

Wicken Fen

Start	Wicken Fen, National Trust car park
Distance	6 miles (9.7km)
Approximate time	3 hours
Parking	National Trust car park
Refreshments	Tearoom at National Trust Visitor Centre, pubs at Upware and Wicken
Ordnance Survey maps	Landranger 154 (Cambridge & Newmarket), Explorer 226 (Ely & Newmarket)

Few areas remain to show what the fens looked like before they were systematically drained to create farmland, but that at Wicken is perhaps the best. The walk skirts the National Trust reserve to meet the River Cam at Upware, returning along Wicken Lode, a channel probably dug by the Romans. Keep your eyes open for koniks, which are related to the tarpan, a small wild horse from the Russian steppes and used to help manage the fenland vegetation.

Wicken Fen (telephone 01353 720274; www.wicken.org.uk) is the country's oldest nature reserve, acquired by the National Trust in 1899 to preserve something of this ancient and richly rewarding waterscape. An abundance of fish and waterfowl provided a living for early inhabitants, whose settlements were protected from both land and sea by the extensive marshes. This small area of wetland habitat still teams with life, the pools and channels full of invertebrates and fish. Dragonflies, damselflies and butterflies fill the air during early summer, whilst many waterbirds over-winter on the water. Other birds you might see include warblers, sparrowhawks and hen harriers and the list of plants and sedges is extensive. There are a number of hides within the reserve and the Visitor Centre contains interesting displays describing the ecology and wildlife of the fen.

🥾 From the car park, go left towards the Visitor Centre, but then

almost immediately turn off right to follow Breed Fen Drove away from the lane. As the track later swings within the field corner, cross a stile just before a gate on the left **Ⓐ**. Head away along a raised bank, Spinney Drove at the edge of the reserve, continuing beyond it to emerge onto a lane, Upware Road. Cross diagonally right and strike out across the field opposite. Passing an encroaching corner, keep going beside the hedge, leaving through a gap at the far side onto a grass track **Ⓑ**.

Follow it left past a wood into another field. Turning right, follow the edge around to remain within the field, paralleling the course of the as yet unseen River Cam. Through a kissing-gate just left of the far corner, cross a meadow to emerge over a footbridge onto a lane at Upware **Ⓒ**.

Go right and then wind left past the front of the Five Miles riverside pub, continuing, not on the grassy waterside sward, but remaining on the embankment above the river, marked The Fen Rivers Way. Meeting another lane, turn right past a former pumping station to a bridge across Reach Lock, there leaving left along a path beside Reach Lode **Ⓓ**.

Shortly, after crossing a footbridge over Wicken Lode, go left again, following the ancient channel bounding the Wicken Fen Nature Reserve. After a mile (1.6km) the waterway splits, the path bearing right beside Monk's Lode. Eventually reaching the edge of the fen **Ⓔ**, cross the drain at a gated bridge and turn right along a path towards the village of Wicken.

To reach the pub, keep ahead as it develops into a lane at the end. Otherwise, go left before the first of the houses following the field perimeter. Pass out through a kissing-gate part-way along and continue on a contained path that leads past the foot of a windmill. Carry on over a crossing drive, later joining a tarmac track. Eventually meeting a lane, turn left back to the car park. ●

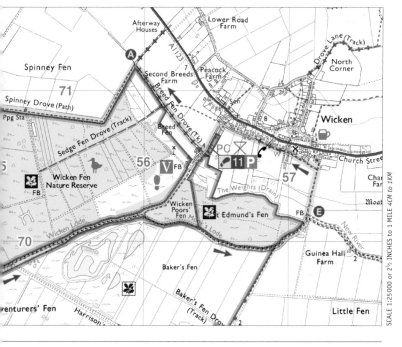

St Ives, Houghton and the Hemingfords

Start	St Ives
Distance	6 miles (9.7km)
Approximate time	3 hours
Parking	St Ives
Refreshments	Pubs and cafés at St Ives, pub at Houghton, café at Houghton Mill, pub at Hemingford Abbots, pub at Hemingford Grey
Ordnance Survey maps	Landranger 153 (Bedford & Huntingdon, St Neots & Biggleswade), Explorer 225 (Huntingdon & St Ives)

This classic, relaxing and highly enjoyable riverside walk in the valley of the Great Ouse has just about everything: attractive town, unusual medieval bridge, three exceptionally pretty villages, complete with thatched cottages, impressive medieval churches and appealing pubs, an old mill, a Norman manor house and gardens, woodland and lush meadows. The route is punctuated by the slender church spires that rise above the flat landscape. Choose a fine day, take your time and enjoy it to the full.

St Ives stands on the north side of the Great Ouse, which is crossed by an impressive 15th-century six-arched bridge. It possesses one of only four surviving bridge chapels in England, built at the same time as the bridge. The skyline of St Ives is dominated by two tall church spires at either end of the town centre. The parish church of All Saints is a fine example of a large and prosperous 15th-century town church, and its elegant spire has been rebuilt several times, the most recent being in 1923–4, after being hit by an aircraft. The spire of the 19th-century Free Church was deliberately made a few feet higher as an assertion of Victorian nonconformity.

The walk begins in Market Hill by the statue to Oliver Cromwell and near the Free Church. With the church on your left, walk along the road towards the spire of the parish church, later joining the river. Where the road bends right, keep ahead along a tarmac path 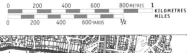 to enter the churchyard and pass to the left of the church. The path curves right to go through a gate onto a road. Head across to a footbridge: do not cross it but bear right, at an Ouse Valley Way sign, along an enclosed path (Barnes Walk) beside the River Great Ouse. The route continues in a fairly straight line along this attractive, tree-lined, tarmac path for the next 1½ miles (2.4km), initially by the river and later through Thicket Wood. Finally a lane (Thicket Road) brings you into the village square (the Green) in Houghton ⓑ. Around it are picturesque cottages and a pub, and in the centre is a thatched clock tower.

Turn left along Mill Street to Houghton Mill, passing the mainly 14th-century church. Turn left into the car park and turn right to pass under an arch of the 17th-century, timber watermill, the oldest surviving mill on the Great Ouse and now owned by the National Trust (tel. 01480 301494). After crossing the mill race, the path bends first right, then curves left and finally turns right to cross a footbridge by Houghton Mill Lock. Go through a gate, take the tarmac path ahead across Hemingford Meadow and go through another gate on the far side.

Cross a footbridge over an arm of the river, keep ahead to a T-junction and turn left ⓒ along a road through Hemingford Abbots, another delightful village with an imposing medieval church. The road bends right through the village centre and, just before a junction, you turn left ⓓ at a public footpath sign, beside a thatched black and white cottage, and walk along an enclosed tarmac path to a kissing-gate. Go through; follow a worn path across a field, go through a kissing-gate on the far side and keep ahead along a path through trees to go through another kissing-gate.

Continue along a low embankment above riverside meadows, go through a kissing-gate and keep ahead along a tarmac path beside the Great Ouse to Hemingford Grey. This is a beautiful stretch of the river, with views across meadows to the left and the picture postcard view of the truncated spire of Hemingford Grey church ahead. You also pass to the left of the manor house, allegedly the oldest continuously inhabited house in England, with parts dating back to the 12th century. It has a most attractive garden open to the public.

The path emerges onto the end of a lane; turn left and then turn right at a public footpath sign, along an enclosed riverside path to the medieval church. The reason for the unusual spire is that it was destroyed by a hurricane in 1741 and what was left was levelled off.

Turn right into the village along a most attractive lane and, at a public footpath sign, turn left **E** along an enclosed path (Love Lane), which emerges, via a barrier, onto a lane. Keep ahead and, where the lane ends, go through a hedge gap beside a gate and bear right to go through a kissing-gate into Hemingford Meadow. This is managed as a traditional hay meadow and is rich in both wildlife and wild flowers.

As you walk along the right-hand edge of the meadow, there are lovely views across it to St Ives. The path later veers slightly left, away from the edge, and heads across to a gate on the far side. Go through, pass under an arch of a hotel complex and keep ahead beside the Dolphin Hotel to a road **F**. Turn left to cross St Ives Bridge, keep ahead along Bridge Street to a T-junction and turn right, back to the starting point. ●

The Great Ouse at Hemingford Grey

Wansford, Sutton, Upton and Thornhaugh

Start	Wansford Bridge
Distance	8 miles (12.9km)
Approximate time	4½ hours
Parking	Roadside parking in village
Ordnance Survey maps	Landranger 142 (Peterborough), Explorer 227 (Peterborough)

After meandering through water meadows beside the River Nene to Sutton, the walk follows quiet lanes to Upton. The return favours higher ground, passing Sacrewell Farm and Country Centre to Thornhaugh before finally dropping through fields and old meadows back the medieval bridge at Wansford.

A fine old bridge unites the two halves of Wansford, striding across the River Nene in a succession of graceful arches. Overlooking all is St Mary's Church, dating from Saxon times but with a later broach spire characteristic of the area. For much of its history the church was without a chancel and then claimed to be the smallest parish church in England, just 30 by 25½ feet (9.1 by 7.7m). Amongst its treasures is a beautifully carved Norman font, discovered at nearby Sibberton Lodge where it did duty as a cattle trough.

From the Haycock Hotel, cross Wansford Bridge and, at a junction by the church, go right. Just before the main road, look for a concrete track dropping right, marked as the Nene Way. Wind beneath the twin road bridges and climb to a rest area **A**. Follow the service road right, but where it swings to the main road, leave right on the continuing Nene Way. Over a stile beyond a fringe of bushes, skirt a field to a second stile and wander to the river.

Accompany the bank downstream through a succession of riverside meadows. After almost ³⁄₄ mile (1.2km), the path swings up between fences to run beside a wood. Follow the developing track until the way is barred by a gate, to the right of which is a kissing-gate. Slip through to continue in the adjacent field and then along an

The small church at Upton

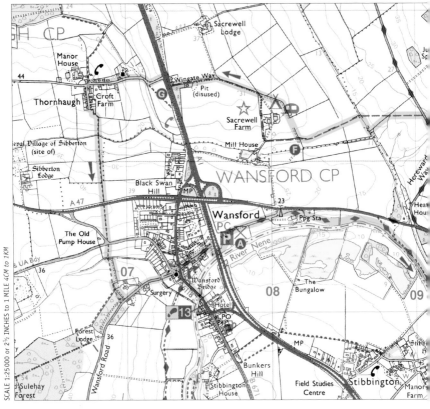

enclosed path, shortly meeting a lane in Sutton **B**.

Turn left past the 12th-century church and over a disused railway, walking beyond the village to a T-junction. Go left to a roundabout on the busy main road **C**, carefully crossing to the continuing lane opposite. Signed to Upton, it rises gently through open countryside. Just

The River Nene near Wansford

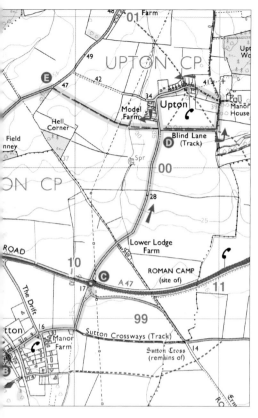

away, continuing beside subsequent fields and eventually reaching a lane **E**. Head left and then, at a junction, right, walking on for some 250 yds (229m) before leaving through consecutive waymarked gates on the left. Just ahead, turn through another gate on the right, and follow the left-hand fence away. Entering a large crop field, drop left around the perimeter to a footbridge, partway along the bottom boundary. Climb away with the hedge on your right, meeting a tarmac drive at the top **F**, which to the right, leads past Sacrewell Farm.

Skirt a camping field and then bear right between open fields. At a later fork keep left, shortly entering trees before meeting the A1 **G**.

Carefully cross the dual carriageway through a gap in the crash barrier and take the lane opposite into Thornhaugh. In the village, go left along Meadow Lane entering the field at its end. Follow the left perimeter down to a footbridge and climb away with a high hedge on your left.

Meeting a main road at the top, cross to a stile opposite and carry on across a sloping meadow. Emerging through trees at the bottom at a junction of lanes, cross to a stile. Strike out across another old meadow and, over a bridge, head up beside a small plantation of saplings. Reaching the edge of a mature wood, look for a waymarked path into the trees. It winds through to Wansford Road, which to the left returns you to Wansford's church. ●

before reaching Model Farm at the top of the hill **D**, leave right through a gap into the field. Doglegging left, follow a grass bridleway that runs between trees and a hedge, Blind Lane. At the end, go left, soon emerging onto a metalled track by Manor House. Grassy mounds betray the site of the medieval village that surrounded the now isolated church, which was extended to accommodate the private chapel and lavish burial vault of the lords of the manor. Closer to, a curiously carved stone stands in a small paddock, an elaborate 17th-century sundial.

Turn left through the present village, keeping left again past Model Farm back to point **D**. Now, cross the stile on the right and accompany the field edge

Stilton and Folksworth

Start	Stilton
Distance	6 miles (9.7km)
Approximate time	3 hours
Parking	Roadside parking at Stilton
Refreshments	Pubs at Stilton, pub at Folksworth
Ordnance Survey maps	Landranger 142 (Peterborough), Explorer 227 (Peterborough)

From Stilton, the walk takes you on a circuit of pleasant, gently rolling countryside just to the south of Peterborough. There are fine views, attractive wooded stretches, and the route passes the site of the deserted medieval village of Washingley and its motte-and-bailey castle.

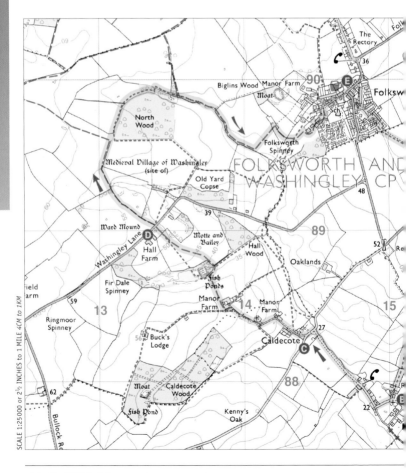

SCALE 1:25 000 or 2½ INCHES to 1 MILE 4CM to 1KM

Until bypassed, Stilton was situated on the Great North Road; hence the wide main street and collection of old coaching inns. This also explains why it has given its name to the best-known of English blue cheeses, which was produced farther west, mostly in Leicestershire, but marketed and distributed here. The mainly 13th-century church is dominated by its tall, Perpendicular tower.

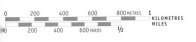 Start in the centre of the village at the junction of High Street and Church Street and walk along Church Street, passing to the right of the church. Where the road bends right Ⓐ, keep ahead, first along a lane and then

a track. Just before reaching a cottage, bear left and climb a stile into a field. Head gently uphill, climb a stile, continue in the same direction across the next field and, on the far side, go through a hedge gap and cross a plank footbridge.

Walk across a field, bear slightly left to continue across the next field, making for a stile, and, after climbing it, keep along the right-hand edge of a field, bearing left away from it to a gate. Go through, keep ahead across a narrow field towards a farm, climb a stile and walk through the farmyard to a lane Ⓑ.

Turn right: at a T-junction turn right again and, at the next T-junction in the hamlet of Caldecote, turn left along a lane signposted to The Giddings.

At a fork, take the right-hand lane Ⓒ gently uphill to a converted Victorian church. At this point the lane becomes a track. Keep along it to a public footpath sign, turn left along another track and, at a public bridleway sign, turn right, initially along the right-hand edge of a field. Follow a grassy track across the field and, on the far side, turn right along its bottom edge. The field edge curves left to a waymarked post. Turn left to cross a brook, keep ahead to go through a gate and bear left to follow an obvious worn track across a field, curving right to a stile. To the right is the site of a motte-and-bailey castle, little more than a low mound and probably constructed in Stephen's reign, around the middle of the 12th century.

Climb the stile, keep ahead across grass to join a tarmac drive and follow it between stone gateposts onto a lane Ⓓ. Cross over and take the track opposite along the right-hand edge of a field. Bumps in the field on the right are all that remains of the medieval village of Washingley. It is likely that it became

Thatched cottage near Stilton

deserted in the 14th century as a result of the Black Death.

Keep ahead to cross a footbridge, continue along the right-hand edge of the next field, curving right and heading gently uphill and, in the field corner, turn right over a stile. Cross a plank footbridge and keep ahead to the corner of North Wood.

Turn left over another plank foot-bridge and keep along the left-hand edge of the wood. At a waymarked post, follow the path into the wood. After fording a brook, turn left and cross a plank footbridge to emerge from the trees. Turn right to walk along the left-hand edge of the wood again. In the field corner keep ahead through a belt of trees and continue along the right-hand edge of a field. Turn left in the corner to continue along the field edge and, at the next corner, turn right through a gate and walk along the left-hand edge of the next field to another

gate. After going through that one, continue along a track that curves left towards the houses of Folksworth, turns right through a gate, curves left through another gate and emerges onto a road.

Turn right and, at a T-junction, turn left along a road, which bends right into the village, passing the Fox pub. Turn right Ⓔ into Washingley Road and, at a public footpath sign, turn left onto a tarmac path between houses. At a fork, take the right-hand path to emerge onto a road: keep ahead and, just before a T-junction, bear right along a tarmac path by the right-hand edge of a green. Cross Townsend Way and keep ahead to climb a stile into a field.

Bear slightly left and head in a straight line across the field to a stile on the far side. Climb it, continue diagonally across the next field in the direction of Stilton church tower and, in the far corner, climb a stile onto a road. Turn left into Stilton, turn right at a T-junction, and the road bends left to return to the start.

Lolworth, Knapwell and Boxworth

Start	Lolworth
Distance	6 miles (9.7km)
Approximate time	3 hours
Parking	Roadside parking at Lolworth; please do not park on the Green
Refreshments	Pub at Boxworth
Ordnance Survey maps	Landranger 154 (Cambridge & Newmarket), Explorer 225 (Huntingdon & St Ives)

The walk takes you across gently undulating terrain to the south of the River Great Ouse and passes through three quiet and attractive villages, all with fine medieval churches. The walking is easy and there are wide views over the surrounding countryside.

Lolworth's mainly 14th-century church lies a little to the north of the village centre.

Start by the crossroads on the Green and walk southwards along High Street. Where the tarmac lane ends, keep ahead along a wide, straight, hedge-lined grassy track to a gate.

Go through, walk along the right-hand edge of a field and, at a waymarked post just before reaching the corner, bear left and head across to a gate Ⓐ.

Ahead are farm buildings and Childerley Hall, and, beyond that, the site of a deserted medieval village. After going through the gate, bear right

The castellated church at Boxworth

Near Lolworth

across grass to a tarmac track; turn right and follow the track around several bends. Look out for a yellow-waymarked post where you turn left along the left-hand edge of a field. Keep ahead through a hedge gap in the corner, walk along the right-hand edge of the next field and continue along a straight tarmac track to a lane.

Cross over, continue along the enclosed, pleasantly tree-lined track opposite for ¾ miles (1.2km) to a road **B** and turn right into Knapwell. At public footpath signs to Boxworth and Knapwell Church, turn right **C** along a tree-lined track, which passes to the left of the small church. The church has a 15th-century tower, the rest was mainly rebuilt in the Victorian period. Go through a kissing-gate, continue along an enclosed path, cross a footbridge, ascend steps and walk across a field, making for the corner of woodland.

Keep by the right-hand edge of the field, along the edge of Overhall Grove and, about 100 yds (91m) before the field corner, turn left across the field to the edge of another belt of trees (Overhall Spinney). Continue along the right-hand edge of the trees to climb a stile and turn right along the right-hand edge of a field. Cross a concrete track,

continue along the right-hand field edge and, just before the corner, turn right through a hedge gap and turn left to a stile. Climb it, keep ahead along an enclosed, grassy track and climb another stile onto a lane **D**.

Turn left, and the lane bends right to a T-junction in front of the Golden Ball at Boxworth. Turn right along High Street and, at a public footpath sign, turn left through a gate and walk

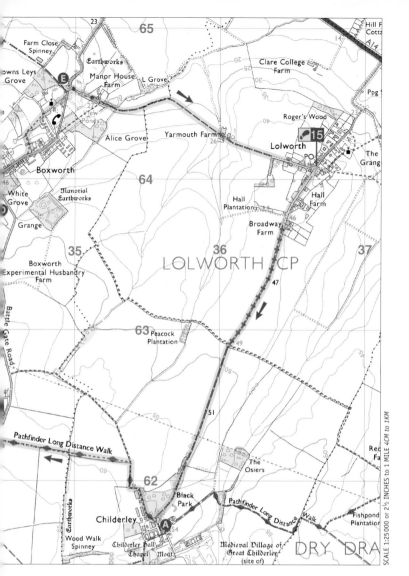

diagonally across a field, making for a gate in the right-hand corner. Go through, keep along the right-hand edge of a field and, where it shortly bends right, turn half-right and head across the field, making for a fence corner. Continue by the fence to go through a gate, cross a track and take the tarmac path along the right-hand edge of Boxworth churchyard. Over to the left is a fine view of the battlemented medieval church.

Turn right through a kissing-gate and turn left along a narrow lane to a road.

Turn left and, at a public bridleway sign to Lolworth, turn right **E** along a tarmac track (Manor Lane). Where the tarmac ends, keep ahead along a track, which is enclosed at first and then continues along the left-hand edge of fields. The track later bears right and heads across fields towards a farm.

Keep ahead between the farm buildings along a gently ascending concrete track, which continues along the right-hand edge of a field and emerges onto a lane. Keep ahead into Lolworth.

St Neots and Little Paxton

Start	St Neots, Riverside Park
Distance	7¼ miles (11.7km)
Approximate time	3½ hours
Parking	Riverside Park car park
Refreshments	Pubs and cafés at St Neots, pub at Little Paxton and refreshments at Paxton Pits Nature Reserve Visitor Centre
Ordnance Survey maps	Landranger 153 (Bedford & Huntingdon), Explorer 225 (Huntingdon & St Ives)

Beginning from St Neots' spacious riverside park, the walk follows the River Great Ouse north to an extensive nature reserve that has grown up around the abandoned pits of sand and gravel workings. For those with time to spare, several marked trails explore the area in greater detail and the Visitor Centre contains a wealth of information on the reserve's history and wildlife.

Founded in 974, Eynesbury Priory stood on the east bank of the river, just north of the bridge, and brought prosperity to the town after the remains of St Neot, a monk from Glastonbury Abbey, were buried there. Abandoned at the Dissolution, there is now no trace of the monastery, but the memory of the saint was perpetuated when the town changed its name.

From the corner of the car park by St Neots Bridge, pass beneath and climb steps to the road. Cross the river and immediately turn off beside The Bridge House along The Priory. Take the next right, which leads past a couple of car parks, leaving between them at a sign for the Ouse Valley Way. Cross a street at the far side and keep ahead down a passage, crossing another street to continue along a short track to reach a concrete drive **A**.

To the left, it leads to the Ouse Valley Rowing Club, but just before the gate, leave over a stile on the right. Walk away at the edge of an open field to a gate and turn through into the adjacent Lammas Meadow. Lammas meadows were an important feature of medieval village economy, for although the growing crop was reserved for householders, commoners were allowed to graze their livestock on the stubble after Lammas Day, the traditional harvest. Head across to the River Great Ouse and follow the bank downstream. At the far end, a fence ushers you away from the river to a gate. Passing through, continue beside a ditch at the edge of Islands Common, eventually reaching a road **B**.

Go left past a junction, crossing to an elevated walkway that straddles the twin arms of the river. Gaining the far bank, turn right onto a tarmac path behind houses. Through gates carry on past a small housing estate and, where the path later swings away, walk

0	200	400	600	800 METRES	1	
						KILOMETRE
						MILES
0	200	400	600 YARDS	½		

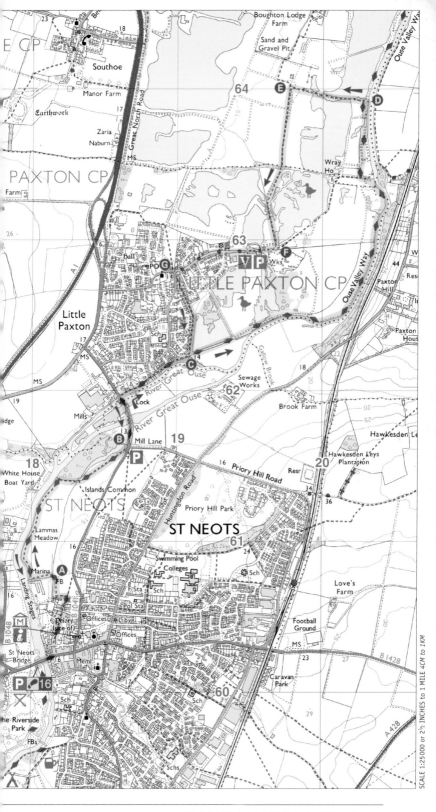

forward over grass to a gate at the edge of the Paxton Pits Nature Reserve Ⓒ.

Still marked 'Ouse Valley Way', a wooded path leads through the reserve, offering brief glimpses of the pools and river on either side. Keep ahead until the path splits at the edge of more open ground and take the right-hand branch, which borders a rough meadow beside the tree-lined river. Reaching the far side, the path curves from the water to a crossing track. Go right, skirting a tangle of wetland wood. Shortly, a brief deviation is justified where a riverside viewpoint is signed off into the trees.

Returning to the main path, walk on to another fork and again go right. After passing moorings, a gate opens into more woodland. Carry on a little farther, but at the next junction Ⓓ, leave the Ouse Valley Way and follow a path left. Reaching the edge of a working gravel pit, the path continues across two service roads. Turn left beside the second Ⓔ and follow it away, later joining the track. Leave through a barrier and turn right past the Visitor Centre Ⓕ.

As the track then forks keep left and continue along a residential street into Little Paxton. After passing The Anchor, take the second turning on the left, Gordon Street Ⓖ. A few yards along, a gravel path branches left behind the houses. Later, bear right past a gate into the reserve and continue beside a lake to a junction where you first entered the reserve Ⓒ. Turn right and retrace your outward route to St Neots. ●

The Great Ouse from St Neots Bridge

Isleham

Start	Isleham
Distance	6½ miles (10.5km)
Approximate time	3 hours
Parking	Roadside parking at Isleham
Refreshments	Pubs and café at Isleham
Ordnance Survey maps	Landrangers 143 (Ely & Wisbech) and 154 (Cambridge & Newmarket), Explorer 226 (Ely & Newmarket)

This Fenland walk explores the country to the south and west of Isleham, using a combination of tracks, field paths, quiet lanes and a section of a disued railway track. The views are extensive, and for much of the way the tower and spire of Isleham's impressive church are in sight.

As its name suggests, Isleham grew up on one of the low islands of slightly higher ground that rise above the Fens. The large and spacious cruciform church is particularly impressive in such a small village. It dates mainly from the 14th century, though the west tower and spire had to be rebuilt in

1863 following the collapse of its predecessor. Nearby is the simple and plain Norman church of a small Benedictine priory, built in the late 11th century. It was suppressed in 1414 at the time of the Hundred Years War because it was an alien priory, belonging to an enemy (French) abbey.

🖊 The walk starts in front of Isleham Priory. With your back to it,

Isleham Priory

turn right and turn right again along West Street. Turn left at a T-junction and turn right at the next T-junction **A**.

Just before a slight rise, bear right along a track **B** – there is an Isleham Society Nature Reserve notice here – which bends right. Pass beside a barrier and continue along a hedge-lined path. This is the track of the disused Cambridge to Mildenhall Railway, opened in 1885 and closed down in the 1960s. Part of it is leased to the Isleham Society as a nature reserve, which is particularly rich in wild flowers.

On emerging from a cutting, keep ahead along an enclosed path, between a fence on the right and a hedge on the left and, at the fence corner, continue along the left-hand edge of a field. In front of a bridge, turn left along the right-hand field edge and turn right onto a narrow lane **C**.

Turn right again, cross the disused railway bridge and follow the lane for one mile (1.6km) to where it ends at Moor Farm. Go through a gate, keep ahead to a public footpath sign by the corner of a barn and follow the track to the left. The track bends right alongside a stream on the left, and you continue along it, negotiating a series of gates and stiles and keeping along the left-hand edge of fields.

After climbing a yellow-waymarked stile, turn right to enter a field; follow a straight path across it and cross a footbridge over a drain onto a road **D**.

Lane near Isleham

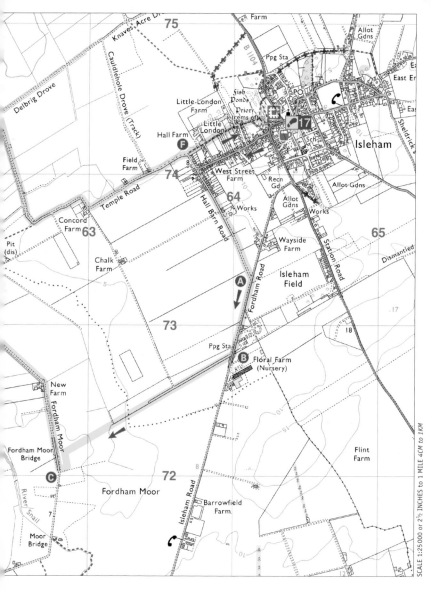

SCALE 1:25000 or 2½ INCHES to 1 MILE 4CM to 1KM

Turn right, at a T-junction turn right again and, where the road turns left, keep ahead **E** along a straight, narrow lane. Follow the lane around left, right and left bends and, where it bends right again on the edge of Isleham, keep ahead **F**, at a public footpath sign, along a concrete drive. Where the drive bends left, keep ahead along a grassy path – there are plenty of waymarks – cross a drive and continue to a gate.

Go through, walk along the right-hand edge of a field, by a line of fine old beeches, go through a gate in the corner and keep ahead along a lane. Where it bends right, continue along an enclosed path to go through a kissing-gate, and Isleham church tower is ahead and the priory to the right. Bear right across a field towards the priory and go through another kissing-gate to return to the starting point in the village of Isleham.

●

Willingham and the Great Ouse

Start	Willingham
Distance	6½ miles (10.5km)
Approximate time	3 hours
Parking	Roadside parking at Willingham, near the church
Refreshments	Pubs at Willingham
Ordnance Survey maps	Landranger 154 (Cambridge & Newmarket), Explorer 225 (Huntingdon & St Ives)

Much of the walking is along the wide, straight drove roads, characteristic of the Fenland landscape, but the middle stretch is along an embankment above the placid waters of the Great Ouse. The church tower at Willingham can be seen throughout most of the second half of the route.

Willingham's large and imposing 14th-century church is noted for its wall-paintings and superb hammerbeam roof.

🥾 Start in the village centre, near the church, at the junction of High Street, Church Street and George Street and walk along George Street, in the Earith and St Ives direction. At a fork, continue along the right-hand main

The Great Ouse near Willingham

road and, after nearly ¹/₂ mile (800m), turn right **Ⓐ**, at a public bridleway sign, along a hedge-and tree-lined track.

The track – appropriately named Flat Road – bends left and continues in a straight line to a T-junction. Turn left along a concrete track, which bends right, and keep along it to where it rises slightly, just before it crosses the river. Turn right over a stile **Ⓑ**, and for the next 1¹/₂ miles (2.4km) the route continues along the top of an embankment above the Great Ouse, climbing a series of stiles. The views – both along the river and across the fens on both sides – are very impressive.

After descending from the embankment, you turn right **Ⓒ** along a track, which keeps along the right-hand edge of fields. This is Aldreth Causeway, an ancient routeway across the Fens, and you follow this wide, green drove to a lane. Keep ahead and, where the lane bends right, keep ahead along an enclosed track to the next lane **Ⓓ**.

Turn right and follow the lane back to the village of Willingham. Keep ahead at a crossroads to return to the starting point. ●

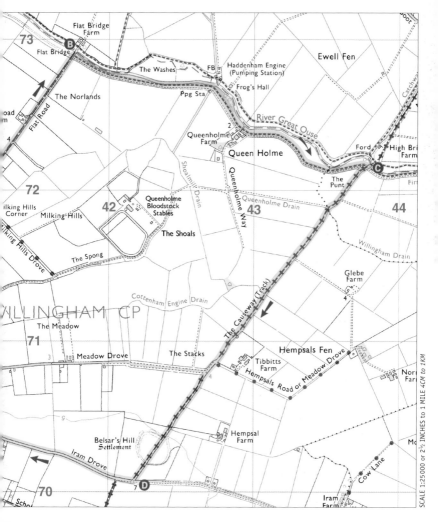

Ely and Little Thetford

Start	Ely Tourist Information Centre
Distance	7 miles (11.3km)
Approximate time	3½ hours
Parking	Ely
Refreshments	Pubs and cafés at Ely
Ordnance Survey maps	Landranger 143 (Ely & Wisbech), Explorer 226 (Ely & Newmarket)

Once a remote island deep in the marshes, Ely's fascinating history justifies a visit in its own right. This pleasant walk across the fields to Little Thetford returns along the banks of the Great River Ouse and reveals the character of today's surrounding landscape, yet leaves ample time to explore the cathedral and discover something of the town's past.

Ely's story begins in the 7th century with the founding of a double monastery by Ethelreda, a Saxon princess. After the death of her first husband, who gave her the island, she married Ecgfrith, the future King of Northumbria, but then turned her back on secular life and retired to a nunnery at Coldingham. Her piety attracted a following and in 672 she established a small community of monks and nuns on the island. She ruled as abbess until her death seven years later, but her reputation persisted and the place eventually became a focus of pilgrimage. The austere Benedictine rule demanded both physical labour and spiritual devotion and the monks became celebrated for their singing. A fragment of an 11th-century ditty has survived, recalling a visit by King Canute:

'Merrily sang the monks of Ely,
As Canute the King rode by.
Row nearer the land knights,
And let us hear these monks sing'

But the Norman invasion clouded such carefree days, the tide of conquest being resisted in many places. Perhaps the most famous rebel was Hereward, a Lincolnshire thane who passed from history into myth after holding out at Ely against William's forces. Immortalised in Charles Kingsley's 19th-century novel, he had sacked Peterborough Abbey in protest against the appointment of a Norman bishop. When defeat seemed inevitable in 1071, he vanished into the fens and whispered stories of his subsequent exploits fanned the sparks of a legend.

The Normans consolidated their position with a motte-and-bailey and in 1080 began a new cathedral, which became known as the 'Ship of the Fens'. It is a truly impressive building with a nave the fourth largest of any English cathedral. A beautifully painted wooden ceiling is carried on soaring pillars, but even more magnificent is the unique octagon and lantern soaring above the transept. Replacing the original central tower that fell down in 1322, it is a feat

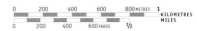

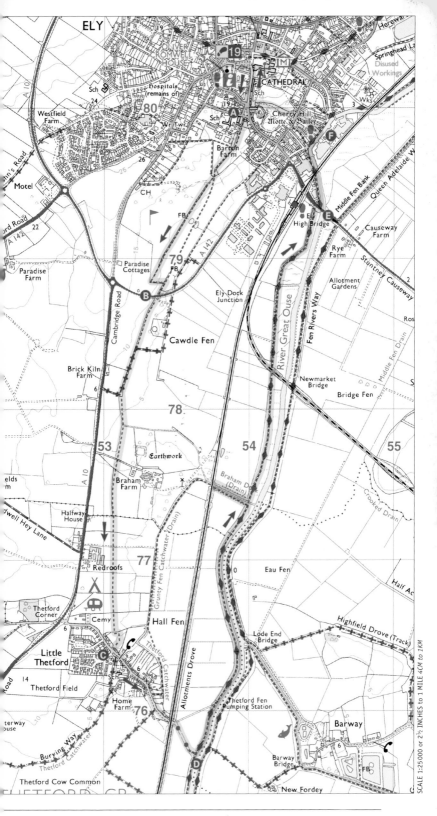

SCALE 1:25000 or 2½ INCHES to 1 MILE 4CM to 1KM

Ely Cathedral

of medieval ingenuity and craftsmanship. Tragedy struck again in the 15th century with the collapse of the northern aisle, bringing down with it the ornate façade and turrets flanking the western portal. Impressive too are the Bishop's Palace and buildings that became the old grammar school founded by Henry VIII, which incorporate a fine old gateway, known as the Ely Porta.

🖉 Leaving the Tourist Information Centre, for a time home to Oliver Cromwell, bear right past St Mary's Church to the cathedral. In front go right along The Gallery and over a mini-roundabout to a small triangular green. Cross ahead to a drive, marked as a footpath and leading to the King's School visitors' car park Ⓐ. As it turns, keep forward across playing fields and an assault course, the way signed to Little Thetford and defined by occasional wayposts. Curving left at the far side, pass through a gate onto a golf course.

To the right the onward path, confirmed by sporadic markers, strikes a beeline line between the greens. Reaching the other side, follow a hedge left to cross a ditch and then swing right beside a final tee. Leave through a clump of trees onto a busy road Ⓑ.

Carefully cross to a half-hidden footpath, just right of the entrance drive to Ely Water Treatment Works. Skirt the tree-lined perimeter of the plant, joining a track through a gate. Continue forward along a narrow copse dividing the fields. Where the track later swings right, keep ahead into the corner of a field and carry on by the hedge.

Eventually, over stiles, go over a track to Braham Farm, maintaining your direction across a narrow meadow beyond to another stile. The way continues in an almost straight line through successive fields, later crossing another track by large agricultural buildings. In the final field, bear left towards a small wood, where a gap leads into the bordering trees. A path runs to the left before turning beside a fence, soon leading to a gravel track. Follow it out to the lane in Little Thetford Ⓒ.

Turn left, passing the small church dedicated to St Andrew, its plain interior brightened by an old octagonal font, four faces of which bear protruding carved heads. At the far end of the village, carefully cross an unmanned level crossing where lights warn of coming trains. A track winds on between the fields to the River Great Ouse Ⓓ. Climb onto the embankment and, over a stile, follow it left towards Ely. After one mile (1.6km), the path is forced away from the main flow by a broad ditch, known as Braham Dock, crossing its head beside the railway before returning to the river.

Later on, cross another railway line and carry on along the top of the dike, eventually leaving the fields behind to pass a sports ground. Emerging onto a road Ⓔ, cross to the continuing waterside path and keep on past boat moorings and then beneath a railway bridge. Remain with the pleasant riverside walk as it swings below the Cutter Inn, turning away just beyond Ⓕ to go through Jubilee Park. Reaching the road, cross to a gateway opposite, from which a path winds through Cherry Hill Park, giving a splendid view of the cathedral and passing below the site of the castle. Leave at the far side through the Ely Porta and, turning right, retrace your steps to the start. ●

Wimblington and Stonea Camp

Start	Wimblington, by the church
Distance	7½ miles (12.1km)
Approximate time	3½ hours
Parking	Roadside parking at Wimblington
Refreshments	Pub at Wimblington
Ordnance Survey maps	Landranger 143 (Ely & Wisbech), Explorer 228 (March & Ely)

This is the archetypal Fenland walk, with wide skies and vast and seemingly endless vistas over a totally flat landscape. It is a figure-of-eight walk that takes you across Horse Moor and Latches Fen to the extensive and well-defined earthworks of a Roman camp, one of few such remains in the Fens.

The walk begins by Wimblington's Victorian church, at the south end of the village. Take the cul-de-sac to the right of it and, where this ends, cross the busy A141 and keep ahead along Manea Road. At a public byway sign, turn left **Ⓐ** along a tarmac track (Workhouse Drove).

The track continues as a rough one – pleasantly tree-lined in places – and where the main track turns left to a house, keep ahead along an enclosed

Fenland near Wimblington

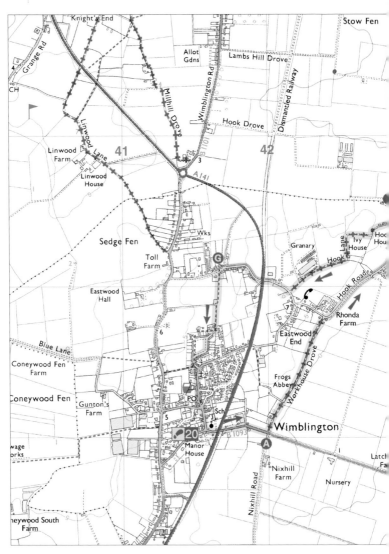

grassy track, which eventually emerges onto a lane. Turn right, follow the lane around a left-hand bend and, where it bends right **B**, keep ahead along a track (Firelots Drove) across the open expanses of Horse Moor. After ¾ mile (1.2km), the track bends right and emerges onto a lane in front of a farm **C**.

Turn right and, at a public footpath sign, turn left onto a path that keeps alongside a drain on the left to a T-junction **D**.

Turn right along a track, which curves left to another T-junction, and turn left along a concrete track. Just after passing a house on the left, look out for a concrete bridge and a footpath sign over to the right. Turn right **E**, walk across a field to cross the bridge, bear left and continue above a drain on the left to reach the well-preserved earthworks and ditches of Stonea Camp **F**.

Access is via a stile. Originally an Iron Age fort, fortified by the Iceni, it was taken over by the Romans and occupied until the 4th century. It was their administrative centre for the Fens

Retrace your steps to the concrete track, turn left **E** and keep along it for

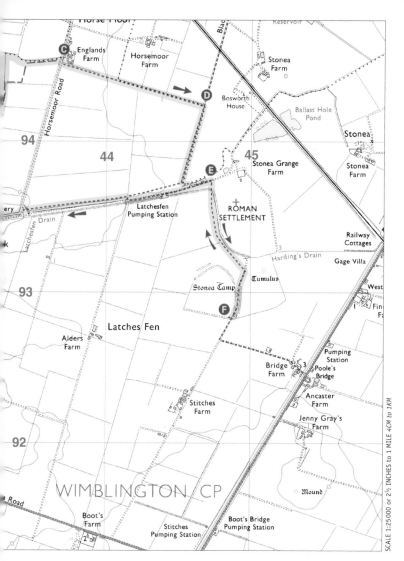

just over one mile (1.6km), eventually bending right to a lane. Turn left; where the lane bends left **B**, you briefly rejoin the outward route, but take the first turning on the right to continue along a tarmac drive. Where the tarmac ends at a public byway sign, bear left along an enclosed track and follow it around several bends, passing a huge granary building. Continue along a tarmac drive to a road and turn right to the A141.

Cross over the road, walk across a grassy strip to the end of a lane and walk along it, following it around a left-hand bend. At a public footpath sign, turn left **G** along an enclosed grassy path, turn right over a footbridge and turn left to continue along an enclosed path to reach a road on the edge of Wimblington. Keep ahead along Hassock Way, turn left along the edge of a large green and follow the road to the right to a T-junction. Turn left and the road curves left to another T-junction. Turn right, passing the Anchor pub and some thatched cottages, to return to the start. ●

Sawtry and the Giddings

Start	Sawtry, St Judith's Lane car park, first road off main street south of post office
Distance	7½ miles (12.1km)
Approximate time	3½ hours
Parking	St Judith's Lane, Sawtry
Refreshments	Pubs at Sawtry, tearoom at Little Gidding
Ordnance Survey maps	Landranger 142 (Peterborough), Explorer 227 (Peterborough)

The walk takes you across a pleasant and undulating landscape on the western fringes of the Fens between Sawtry and the adjacent hamlets of Steeple Gidding and Little Gidding, both of which have interesting churches. On the outward leg, the route passes through part of the delightful and ancient Aversley Wood.

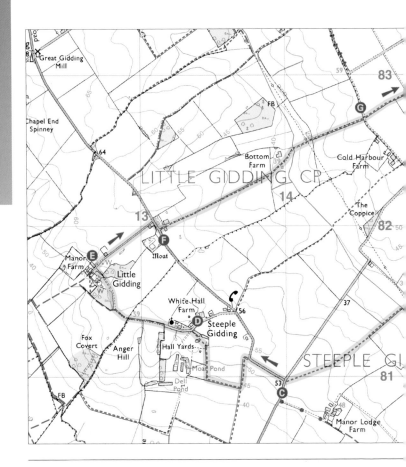

Start by climbing the stile in the car park and head uphill, between a hedge on the right and allotments on the left, to a kissing-gate. Go through and keep along the right-hand edge of a field over the brow of a hill.

The route continues along an undulating, enclosed path by the left-hand edge of Aversley Wood. Descend into a dip, cross a footbridge, head up again and, just after going through a hedge gap, turn right through a gate into the wood **A**; an ancient wood, one of the largest in Cambridgeshire and now owned by the Woodland Trust. At crossways, turn left, keep ahead at the next crossroads and turn right at a T-junction. Turn left at the next T-junction, climb a stile to emerge from the trees and turn right along the edge of the wood.

The track continues across fields to a waymarked post. Turn left **B** along a track towards a farm, continue past the end of the farm buildings to a way-marked post and turn right to a T-junction. Turn left along a tarmac track, follow it around a right-hand bend and, at a waymarked post, turn left onto a grassy track which continues across fields. After crossing a drain, turn right, then almost immediately turn left, continue along a path and cross a plank footbridge. Keep ahead across a large field and go through a hedge gap onto a lane at a junction **C**.

Keep ahead along the lane signposted to The Giddings and, where it bends right, turn left to a public footpath sign

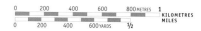

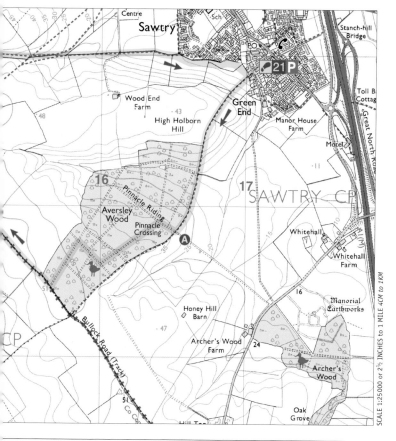

Church at Little Gidding

and turn right along the right-hand edge of a field. After about 20 yds (18m), turn left: turn right over a footbridge, walk along the left-hand edge of a field and turn right in the corner to continue along the left-hand edge and turn left over a stile. Bear right diagonally across the next field, climb a stile onto a lane **D** and turn left into the hamlet of Steeple Gidding, passing the medieval church.

The lane becomes a track that continues across fields and along the right-hand edge of woodland to a T-junction in the equally tiny hamlet of Little Gidding **E**. The church, former farmhouse and other buildings of the community are to the left. A religious community was originally founded here in 1626 by Nicholas Ferrar, and one of its early visitors was King Charles I. T.S. Eliot, was later inspired to write *Little Gidding* as one of his *Four Quartets* (1944). The small brick church dates from the 17th century, with a distinctive stone front added in 1714.

At the T-junction, turn right along a straight, narrow lane to a T-junction, turn right and, at a public footpath sign, turn left **F**, passing in front of barns.

Continue along a winding and undulating track across fields, and pass beside gates onto a lane **G**. Cross over take the path ahead across a field, later keeping along its right-hand edge, then in the corner, follow the path to the left to emerge onto a track. Turn right and, in front of the gate to Woodfield House turn left along the right-hand edge of a field. Cross a track and continue along the right-hand field edge.

Look out for where you turn right through a hedge gap – there is a waymarked post here – you turn left to keep along the left-hand edge of a field and after crossing a footbridge over a ditch the way continues along the right-hand edge of a field again. Another yellow waymark indicates where you turn right again over a footbridge and turn left along the left-hand edge of a field. Just beyond the field corner, turn right over another plank footbridge and turn left to continue along the left-hand edge of the next field, descending gently towards Sawtry.

Cross a track and keep along the left-hand field edge, which finally leads in a recreation ground. Bear right across to return to the start.

Linton, Hildersham and the Roman road

Start	Linton, by the bridge across the River Granta
Distance	7 miles (11.3km)
Approximate time	3¾ hours
Parking	Roadside parking at Linton
Refreshments	Pubs at Linton and Hildersham
Ordnance Survey maps	Landranger 154 (Cambridge & Newmarket), Explorer 209 (Cambridge)

Although hilly by Cambridgeshire's standards, the gradual gradients of this walk should present little difficulty to most people. It climbs from the ancient town of Linton over Rivey Hill to a Roman road, returning by way of Hildersham, where there is an interesting church, along the valley of the River Granta.

Linton's charter dates from 1246 and it remained an important market town until the mid-19th century. It has several fine part-timbered buildings, including the Bell Inn and the medieval Trinity Guild Hall, which stands to the north of the 13th-century church. There are also a number of cottages with façades decorated in attractive plasterwork.

Granta valley near Hildersham

From the bridge across the Granta, follow the main street east through the village. Reaching a junction with the B1052, go left and then, almost immediately, left again. Leave after 200 yds (183m) along a tarred path on the right, a bridleway to Balsham. Passing the cemetery, it later climbs at the edge of Rivey Wood, breaking out by a water tower **A**.

Descend the far side of the hill to a

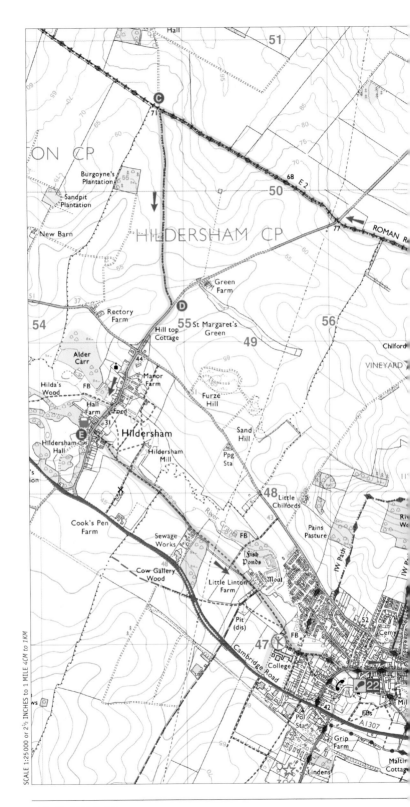

lane and keep ahead past the entrance to Chilford Hall Vineyard. Abandon it a little farther on, slipping through a gap in the right-hand hedge, from which a path, again signed to Balsham, diverges from the lane. Cross two fields, emerging through the top hedge onto the Roman road **B**.

Follow it left, shortly recrossing the lane to continue along the undulating tree-lined route. During the Middle Ages, wool-laden packhorse trains used the track and it became known as Wool Street. The Roman-sounding 'Via Devana' only appeared during the 18th century, when it was thought that the road led all the way to Deva, modern day Chester. After crossing a second lane, carry on for a further mile (1.6km) until the track broadens to a junction **C**.

To the left, a path signed to Hildersham falls between the fields. Meeting a lane **D**, walk along it right to a crossroads and go straight over, dropping past the church. Greatly restored during the 19th century, the chancel walls are richly decorated with colourful murals. Continue across the River Granta to the Pear Tree, turning left immediately after along a short lane signed as a footpath to Linton **E**.

Keep ahead where it finishes into a field, shifting right to a gate in the far corner. Follow the perimeter left, continuing over a track beside successive fields. Where the path forks after passing a water treatment plant, bear left, shortly meeting a junction of tracks. Through a kissing-gate opposite, carry on between paddocks, eventually reaching the village recreation ground. Join a tarmac path along its edge, emerging at the far side onto a short street. At the end, go left back to the bridge spanning the River Granta. ●

0	200	400	600	800 METRES	1
					KILOMETRES MILES
0	200	400	600 YARDS		½

Castor Hanglands

Castor Hanglands

Start	Castor, in main street opposite the church
Distance	7 miles (11.3km)
Approximate time	3½ hours
Parking	Roadside parking at Castor
Refreshments	Pubs at Castor
Ordnance Survey maps	Landranger 142 (Peterborough, Market Deeping & Chatteris), Explorer 227 (Peterborough)

Castor Hanglands is an attractive area of woodland and heath lying to the north of the Nene Valley and just to the west of Peterborough. The first half of the route is mainly across fields and, as there are a number of twists and turns, the route directions need to be heeded carefully. The second half is more straightforward, heading in a fairly straight line through the trees and across the heathland to Ailsworth, the adjacent village to Castor. From here it is a short return to the start.

Castor's superb Norman cruciform church is built on the site of the court-yard of a great Roman palace, and the area was the centre of an extensive pottery industry, producing Castor ware, in Roman times. The church is uniquely dedicated to St Kyneburgha, daughter of Penda, a 7th-century King of Mercia.

Facing the church, turn right and turn left by the Royal Oak along Stocks Hill. Pass to the right of the church and, where the road ends, keep ahead along a track that narrows to an enclosed path. Climb a stile and go up steps to cross the westbound carriageway of the busy A47 Ⓐ.

Turn right along the central reservation to a gap in the barrier, turn left to cross the eastbound carriageway, turn left at a public footpath sign and, at a public bridleway sign, turn right along an enclosed path. Turn left at a T-junction Ⓑ along the left-hand edge

of a field, go through a hedge gap and keep ahead along a track. Where it starts to bear slightly left, turn right at a waymarked post, onto a path that continues along the left-hand edge of fields. At the corner of a young plantation, turn right Ⓒ onto a grassy track, between the plantation on the left and a hedge on the right. The track later curves left and, at a public footpath sign to Castor Hanglands, follow it to the left again, continuing by the right-hand edge of the plantation.

Shortly after the track bears right – and about 50 yds (46m) before it bears right again – turn right along a broad, grassy path across fields. Follow the path around first a left bend, then a right bend Ⓓ and, in the field corner, turn right through a hedge gap and turn left to continue along the right-hand

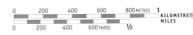

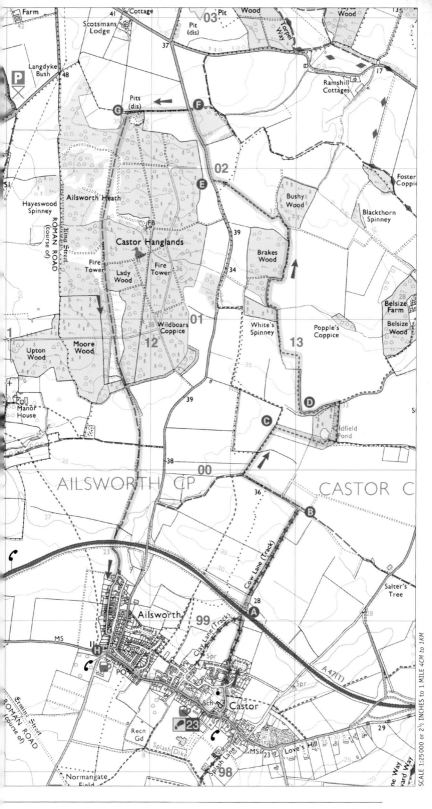

SCALE 1:25000 or 2½ INCHES to 1 MILE 4CM to 1KM

edge of White's Spinney and Brakes Wood. Follow the meandering field edge, keeping by the right-hand edge of the trees all the time and, at the corner of the woodland, keep ahead along the field edge to a T-junction. Turn left along a track – now with woodland on the right – and, at a junction, turn left onto a track that winds between fields to emerge, via a gate, onto a lane **E**.

Turn right and, after just over $^1/_4$ mile (400m), turn left **F** at a public bridle-way sign, along a track. The track runs first along the right-hand edge of a field and later becomes enclosed. At a hedge corner, where there is an English Nature sign 'Castor Hanglands Nature Reserve', turn left through a gate into the reserve **G**.

Castor Hanglands comprises a mixture of woodland and open grass-land. Both are ancient: the woodland is a relic of the former hunting forest of Nassaburgh and the open grassland of Ailsworth Heath was cleared in Saxon times.

Walk along an enclosed path by the right-hand edge of the trees and follow it into the woodland. The well-way-marked route now continues, more or less in a straight line, alternately through woodland and across open heathland, through a series of gates, eventually going through a gate to leave the reserve. As you keep ahead gently downhill along a tree-lined track and then across fields, Castor church spire is seen ahead, and there is a fine view across the Nene Valley. After going through a gate onto an embankment above the A47 again, turn left down to a public footpath sign. Turn right to cross the eastbound carriageway, turn right along the central reservation and turn left to cross the westbound carriageway, heading up steps on the other side to go through a gate.

Continue along an enclosed path to reach a lane on the edge of Ailsworth and keep ahead along it, bending left to a T-junction. Turn right and, at the next T-junction **H**, turn left and follow the road through Ailsworth and back to Castor. ●

Thatched pub at Castor

Gog Magog Hills and the Granta Valley

Start	Wandlebury Country Park
Distance	7 miles (11.3km)
Approximate time	3½ hours
Parking	Wandlebury Country Park car park
Refreshments	Pubs at Stapleford
Ordnance Survey maps	Landranger 154 (Cambridge & Newmarket), Explorer 209 (Cambridge)

Cambridgeshire is not renowned for its hills, but the few places where the ground does significantly rise have always drawn people. The Gog Magog Hills are no exception and betray ancient settlement in the mounds of ancient burials, defensive earthworks and a Roman road. This walk to the nearby village of Stapleford, with its ancient church and pubs, wanders on along the shallow Granta Valley before returning along a pleasant stretch of the undulating Roman highway.

Occupying a commanding position and the site of earlier Stone and Bronze Age settlements, Wandlebury Ring is a fine Iron Age hillfort, defended by a deep encircling ditch and embankment over ½ mile (800m) in circumference. Thrown up in the 3rd century BC, it was reinforced during the 1st century BC and there is evidence of later Roman occupation within the enclosed area. The Anglo Saxons used the spot as a meeting place and gave it the name by which we know it today, Wendlesbiri. James II established a stud here and, in the 1730s, the second Earl Godolphin destroyed much of the ancient ramparts in extending the stables and building a house. He was owner of the famous racehorse *Godolphin Arab,* from which many of today's thoroughbreds are descended. The horse died in 1753 and was buried beneath the cupola in the stables, the only part of the buildings to remain after the house was demolished in the 1950s.

Head back to the dual carriageway and carefully cross to a gated footpath opposite. Go right, signed to Stapleford, as far as an opening on the left some 50 yds (46m) along. Turning in, immediately pass through a narrow gate on the right onto Magog Down. Not necessarily following trods, which perversely ignore the line of the right of way, strike diagonally across the slope of the hill, passing a waypost to a gate at the far bottom corner. A contained path continues through the small plantation of Colin's Wood to emerge onto Haverhill Road Ⓐ. Go left towards Stapleford.

After ¾ mile (1.2km), at the edge of the village, turn right into Gog Magog Way. Follow it to a junction by an

The 'Mile Road' near Wandlebury

eventually reaching a stile in the right-hand fence. Cut the corner of the adjacent field to a bridge and cross the River Granta **D**. Follow a track on for 200 yds (183m) before leaving through a kissing-gate on the left. Take a grass path through a plantation of saplings, going left at a junction in the middle. Recross the river and keep ahead along the left-hand field edge. Later doglegging right and left, resume your heading beside a final field to emerge onto the main road **E**.

Follow the verge right for 200 yds (183m) before crossing to a marked bridleway, Mile Road. It steadily rises in a dead-straight line towards the high

island green, there going left into Bar Lane. After passing Green Hedges School, leave along a tarmac path on the right, Vicarage Lane, which leads through to Church Lane **B**. Built of flint, St Andrew's lies not far to the right. Amongst its interesting features, the church has an early Norman chancel arch, the sides pierced by squints to allow those seated in the aisles a view to the altar. A Saxon grave marker and Norman grave cover are also relics of its early history.

The onward route, however, continues along Church Lane in the other direction, shortly passing a small flint building, a 19th-century slaughter-house, before reaching the main road by The Longbow. Turn left, passing a second pub, The Rose, before going left again into Bury Road. Where it later bends **C**, keep ahead along a track signed to Babraham and Sawston that leads past Bury Farm.

The way courses between open fields for over a mile (1.6km), giving a fine view to the Magog hills. Keep going as the track later narrows to a path,

ground, eventually levelling beside the tree-clad Copley Hill, which is the site of a large Bronze Age burial mound. Turning left at a junction, you are now on Via Devana, an 18th-century name for the Roman road built around AD43 between Colchester and Godmanchester. It falls pleasantly between trees and high hedges, after ¹/₂ mile (800m) reaching two adjacent paths leaving on the left **F**.

Take the second of the two, signed to Wandlebury Ring and Cambridge, passing along a strip of woodland to a

junction in front of a cottage. To the right, the path shortly emerges at the edge of the trees. Keep left where the way later forks, winding on past open space. The obvious track then hugs the tree fringe once more before rising to a tarmac track beside a bridge spanning the surrounding ditch of the ancient hillfort. Turn left back to the car park.

Barnack, Helpston and Ufford

Start	Barnack, by the church
Distance	7½ miles (12.1km)
Approximate time	4 hours
Parking	Roadside parking at Barnack
Refreshments	Pubs at Barnack, Helpston and Ufford
Ordnance Survey maps	Landranger 142 (Peterborough), Explorers 234 (Rutland Water) and 235 (Wisbech & Peterborough North)

At Barnack, the low-lying levels give way to gently rolling hills of limestone, a warm mellow rock that has lent its character to the villages dotting the landscape. However, today's neatly hedged fields and woodland copses, through which the walk meanders, are quite different from the ragged, open heathland remembered by the Helpston poet, John Clare, during the early 19th century.

The splendid building qualities of Barnack's stone were recognised by the Romans and the quarries they began were worked throughout the medieval period. The quarries provided fine ashlar for many churches and cathedrals in the area, its widespread use enabled by the maze of channels and rivers through the fens, along which the cut stone could be transported great distances. Barnack's own church is an impressive example and illustrates the changing architectural styles of the passing centuries. The oldest part, the tower, was raised at the beginning of the 11th century in typically bold Saxon style, the long and short stonework still striking.

John Clare's cottage, Helpston

With the church on your left, follow Main Street through a couple of bends to a T-junction with the B1443. Turn right and walk out of the village. Just after the speed de-restriction sign, a footpath marked the Torpel Way is signed off right **A**. It hugs the field perimeter adjacent to the road and reaching

Barnack church

the corner, swings away within the field. After 50 yds (46m) go left at a waymark along the edge of the adjoining field. Again turn with the corner, then look for a plank bridge spanning the left-hand ditch. Pass through a small wood and continue in the next field. At the far end, accompany the hedge right to the next corner, where a 'Torpel Way' sign to Ashton directs you through a gap on the left. Walk on, finally crossing a footbridge onto a lane. Over a stile breaking the opposite hedge, keep ahead across successive fields. Emerging onto a second lane on the outskirts of Ashton, follow it right to a junction in the village **B**.

Go left, but then immediately leave through a kissing-gate on the right along an enclosed path, again marked 'Torpel Way'. Wind on, eventually entering a crop field. Walk ahead at its edge and then, over a stile, bear right across a couple of paddocks, where grassy mounds and ditches outline a ring and bailey. Pass out at the far side to a junction and follow the main lane ahead to a crossroads in the centre of Helpston **C**.

Born here in 1793, John Clare is celebrated as the 'Peasant Poet'. Put to work tending sheep as a child, throughout his life he developed an intimate understanding and love of the countryside at a time when the rough heath and natural woodland were being tamed by enclosure. Clare's legacy is a

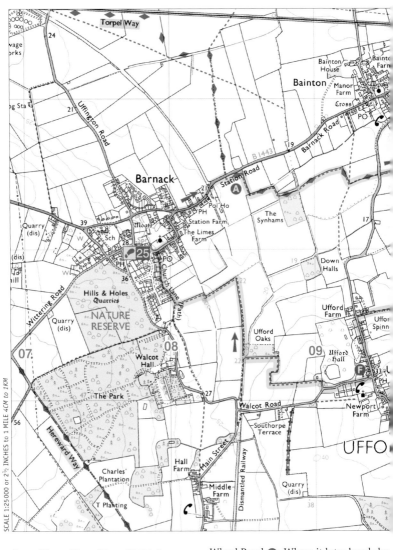

SCALE 1:25000 or 2½ INCHES to 1 MILE 4CM to 1KM

| 0 | 200 | 400 | 600 | 800 METRES | 1 |
| 0 | 200 | 400 | 600 YARDS | ½ |

KILOMETRES
MILES

unique glimpse into that world, not through the eyes of a Romantic, but one whose every day was governed by nature. He is buried in St Botolph's churchyard and remembered in an elaborate memorial of white stone, which stands at the crossroads opposite the village's 14th-century cross.

Go right along Woodgate, passing the cottage in which Clare was born. At the next junction, turn off into Broad

Wheel Road **D**. Where it later bends by the last of the houses, bear off left onto a bridleway across the fields. Later doglegging left and right, continue at the edge of Rice Wood to a junction with the Torpel Way. Turn right and walk out to a lane. A short distance to the right leave through a waymarked gate on the left. After passing the edge of Hilly Wood, the track carries on between open fields to meet another lane **E**.

Follow it left for about ¼ mile (400m) to a waymarked bridge on the right.

Walk away, initially beside a wood and then a hedge. Later slipping through, continue on its opposite flank to emerge at the edge of Ufford. To the left the lane climbs into the village, reaching a junction opposite Ye Olde White Hart **F**. Ufford's church, St Andrew's, stands impressively on top of the hill, and before the Reformation, was a resting place for pilgrims journeying to the Holy shrine at Walsingham.

However, the onward route lies to the right along Walcot Road. At a bend beyond the village, turn off along a short walled track on the right. Approaching the end, go left over a stile beside a house and head away at the field edge. Walk on in the next field, doglegging around its convoluted perimeter to a footbridge in the far-right bottom corner. Emerging onto a field track, a former railway trackbed, follow it right for a little over ¼ mile (400m). At a waymark, go left and, after winding through a clump of trees, carry on at the edge of the next field. Leave at the corner, where a three-way sign directs you right back to Barnack. ●

Ferry Meadows, River Nene and Peterborough

Ferry Meadows, River Nene and Peterborough

Start	Ferry Meadows Country Park Visitor Centre
Distance	10¼ miles (16.5km) - 5½ miles (8.9km) for short walk
Approximate time	5¼ hours - 2¾ hours for short walk
Parking	Car park by Visitor Centre
Refreshments	Café at Visitor Centre, pubs and cafés in Peterborough
Ordnance Survey maps	Landranger 142 (Peterborough), Explorer 227 (Peterborough)

Contained within a sweeping bend of the River Nene, Ferry Meadows Country Park attracts both watersports enthusiasts and nature lovers. This walk explores the park and can be extended along the river into Peterborough to visit the ancient cathedral church and its precincts.

Prior to gravel extraction during the 1970s, the low-lying fields were worked as farmland and osier beds. The abandoned pits subsequently flooded to form a series of lakes, which, together with the surrounding woods and grass

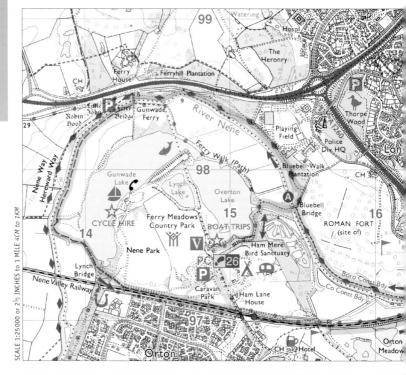

wetlands have attracted a wide range of animal and plant life. The area provides good cover for smaller birds and almost 200 species have been reported.

🖉 Leave the car park beside the Information Centre to a broad track, where the main visitor complex lies to the left. However, keep ahead, picking up a path to Bluebell Wood, which skirts Overton Lake, the water on your left. Over a bridge, turn right, soon crossing a suspension bridge spanning the Nene 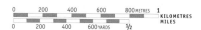Ⓐ.

A short distance beyond, leave the tarmac for a dirt path, delving into Bluebell Wood on the left, signed 'Riverside Walk'. Keep to the lower trail through the trees, later passing restored osier beds worked from the 19th century. Reaching Ferry Bridge, built in 1716 to replace the original ferry, cross and immediately turn through a gate on the right, walking away at the meadow's edge beside the river.

At the far end beyond a drain, the track briefly rejoins the river before

turning away towards Gunwade Lake. Curving right, parallel a cycle track beside the water that shortly leads to a bridge across the Nene Valley Railway. Instead of crossing, continue on a gravel path alongside the railway – part of the line from Northampton to Peterborough, it operated from 1845 until closure in 1972. The section between Wandsford Station and Peterborough was reopened to steam in 1977, worked by both British and continental engines as well as a fully operational mail coach.

Remaining on the path nearest the railway, carry on, later crossing a road. Eventually, at the entrance to Peterborough Yacht Club, cross the line and immediately go left towards Orton Mere. Approaching a car park, keep left and then turn left, crossing the railway and a bridge over Orton Lock Ⓑ.

The quick return heads back upstream

0	200	400	600	800 METRES	1
					KILOMETRES
					MILES
0	200	400	600 YARDS	1/2	

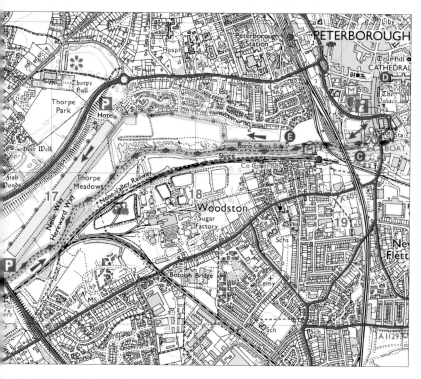

Peterborough Cathedral

to Bluebell Bridge Ⓐ, otherwise carry on to Peterborough following the tarmac cycle path right. As it then swings left, abandon it to pass beneath the road bridge. Staying close to the river, continue on a path beside Thorpe Meadows and later over a bridge, through a local nature reserve. Soon after a second bridge, the path rejoins the cycleway. Carry on beneath successive bridges and then below waterside flats. Reaching a footbridge Ⓒ, turn off the promenade up steps and walk through to a shopping precinct. Almost immediately, at a signpost for the Tourist Information Centre, leave along an alley on the right and keep ahead across a service area to Bridge Street. Turn left, cross over the main road and continue up to Cathedral Square. The cathedral precincts are then reached through a medieval gateway on the right Ⓓ.

Dedicated to the saints Peter, Paul and Andrew, the cathedral stands on a monastic site originally founded by King Paeda in 655. After destruction by Danish raiders in 870, it was rebuilt as a Benedictine abbey, the present church was begun in 1118 following a fire. A truly beautiful building with an exquisitely painted roof, it became a cathedral after the Dissolution in 1541; the last abbot being created its first bishop. Buried here is Catherine of Aragon, Henry VIII's first wife. For a short time after her execution, Mary Queen of Scots lay here too, her body was later reinterred within Westminster Abbey by her son, James I.

Returning to the river, go back along the embankment. However, shortly after passing beneath the last of the bridges leaving the city, bear off with the cycleway Ⓔ following signs to Thorpe Meadow. Reaching a small housing development, swing right over a bridge and then go left towards Orton and Ferry Meadows. After passing the Boat house pub, leave the cycleway and trac the left-hand bank of the Rowing Club lake. Briefly rejoin your outward track beyond its end to pass beneath the road bridge to Orton Lock Ⓑ. Now remaining on this bank, carry on upstream, eventually reaching Bluebell Bridge Ⓐ Cross and retrace your way back to the Visitor Centre and car park.

Ely and Little Downham

Start	Ely, Tourist Information Centre
Distance	10½ miles (16.9km)
Approximate time	5½ hours
Parking	Ely
Refreshments	Pubs and cafés at Ely, pubs at Little Downham
Ordnance Survey maps	Landranger 143 (Ely & Wisbech), Explorer 228 (March & Ely)

It was the small islands of higher ground that attracted settlement within the vast marshes of the Fens, Ely and neighbouring Little Downham being just two examples. This walk between them rambles along old drove roads, where hedges and small copses provide cover for small birds in this open landscape, before finally returning to the town beside the River Great Ouse.

Little Downham has been associated with Ely for over 1,000 years, granted to the monks in 970. During the Middle Ages, the bishops established a summer palace there amidst a 250-acre (101-hectare) deer park, the sparse ruins of which can still be seen just north west of the village.

✐ Leave the Tourist Information Centre along the main road past St Mary's Church, crossing to go left into Downham Road. Very soon, bear left again into West Fen Road and follow it out to the main A10 road. Carefully cross and carry on with the lane opposite, signed to Coveney. After ¼ mile (400m), a byway leaves on the right **A**.

Beyond a barn it continues as a hedged grass track. Reaching a junction, go left on another track, Hurst Lane, then bearing right where it shortly forks. The track runs between the fields towards Little Downham, its dwellings clustered on a low hill. Reaching a house after some 1¼ miles (2km), the onward track becomes metalled and rises to the edge of the village. At a

crossroads, keep ahead up Chapel Lane to Main Street at the top **B**.

Turn right, passing The Anchor to reach St Leonard's Church. In the porch, there is a beautifully carved frieze of human and animal heads surmounting the Norman doorway and, inside, the coat of arms of King George III are believed to be the largest such blazon displayed in any English church. At the village green, keep ahead towards Ely, later going by the brick tower of a windmill, set back from the road. After another ¼ mile (400m), turn left into Marshal Lane **C**, which quickly degrades to a track. Reaching a way-marked junction, go right and, at the end turn left. Keep left again at the subsequent junction and carry on to meet a busy main road.

Take care crossing to the track opposite, which leads to Chettisham **D**. Turn beside its 13th-century church and walk out to the main lane. Go left to a level crossing, immediately over which, leave through a gate on the right onto Kettlesworth Drove **E**. First on one side

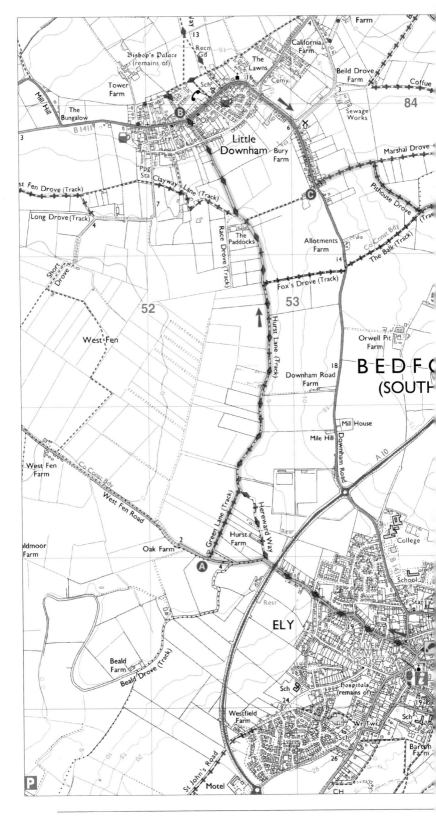

and then the other, follow a meandering ditch across the open, dead-flat fields for a mile (1.6km). Shortly before reaching a second railway line, turn off right onto a grassy track, Clayway Drove **F**.

Watch out for trains as you shortly recross the first railway and carry on to join Prickwillow Road. Follow it ahead for ½ mile (800m), rounding a bend to reach a waymarked metalled track on

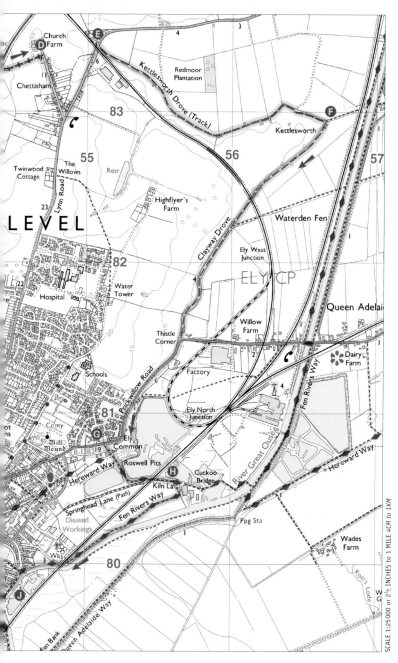

the left **G**. Walk past Environment Agency buildings and between the pools of Roswell Pits Nature Reserve. Beyond another level crossing and just before a small industrial area, look for an 'easy access' trail on the right **H**. Through a gate at its end, strike across a meadow, a developing path soon meeting the River Great Ouse. Beneath a railway bridge, remain with the riverside path to The Maltings, turning off just beyond into Jubilee Park **J**.

Crossing a road at the far side, continue into Cherry Hill Park opposite, from which there is a splendid view across to the cathedral and its majestic crown-like central lantern. Keep ahead through the medieval gateway of the Ely Porta and turn right past the old monastic buildings that became the King's School. Reaching the great west front of the cathedral, swing left across a green to return to St Mary's Church and the Tourist Information Centre.

Drove road near Little Downham

Grafham Water

Start	Grafham Water Visitor Centre, off B661, 1 mile (1.6km) west of Buckden
Distance	9¼ miles (14.9km)
Approximate time	5 hours
Parking	Grafham Water Visitor Centre car park
Refreshments	Pub at Perry, cafés at Visitor Centre and Fishing Lodge
Ordnance Survey maps	Landranger 153 (Bedford & Huntingdon), Explorer 225 (Huntingdon & St Ives)

Built in the 1960s and covering over 1,500 acres, Grafham Water is one of the largest lakes in the region. This walk around its perimeter generally follows a cycle trail, so keep a look out for cyclists, but in the woodland areas, several nature trails offer optional quiet detours through the trees.

The reservoir, the focus of a whole range of outdoor activities, is equally important in offering diverse wildlife habitats and much of the shore has been designated SSSI. The water attracts both migratory and resident wildfowl and there are several hides from which to observe them. Parts of the woodland are centuries old, with coppice management encouraging small birds, mammals and insects and the open meadows are rich in grassland flowers, particularly in spring and early summer.

🖉 Walk towards the lake and follow the shore right. A developing grass path takes the way below a wood and promontory to a junction of paths **A**. Leaving the water's edge through a gate, climb Church Hill to Grafham. All Saints' Church is a short detour to the left. Its rubble construction betrays the scarcity of local stone, but it is still a building of character. Light floods in through high dormer windows and corbelled roof supports are decorated with heads. There is more early carving

in the porch, part of a tomb cover depicting a priest.

Go back along Church Road and turn left into Breach Road, continuing beyond the last of the houses for a further ¼ mile (400m). Signed left **B**, a bridleway follows the field edge towards West Wood. Just before the trees, leave through a broad gap breaking the left-hand hedge and resume your forward direction beside the wood. Keep going in the next field,

Grafham Water

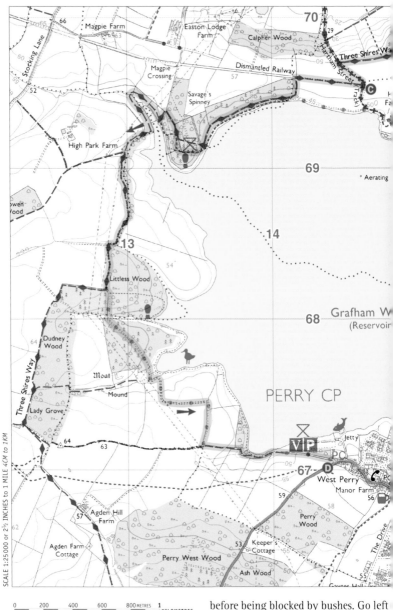

SCALE 1:25000 or 2½ INCHES to 1 MILE 4CM to 1KM

| 0 | 200 | 400 | 600 | 800 METRES | 1 |
| 0 | 200 | 400 | 600 YARDS | ½ |

KILOMETRES
MILES

but at the corner, remain within it, turning left along the boundary to a finger-post **C**.

Bear right into the adjacent field corner, signed 'Grafham Circular Bridleway' and leave onto a grass track. Part of a former railway between Huntingdon and Thrapston, it runs dead straight to the right for ¼ mile (400m)

before being blocked by bushes. Go left and right into the corner of the neighbouring field but as you pass out, look for a waymarked path immediately on the left. Dropping just inside the trees, it breaks out across a strip of flower meadow to the cycle path.

To the right, the track leads through the nature reserve, initially close to the water's edge but soon turning up into the wood. Later emerging, it winds around a small inlet to cross a stream.

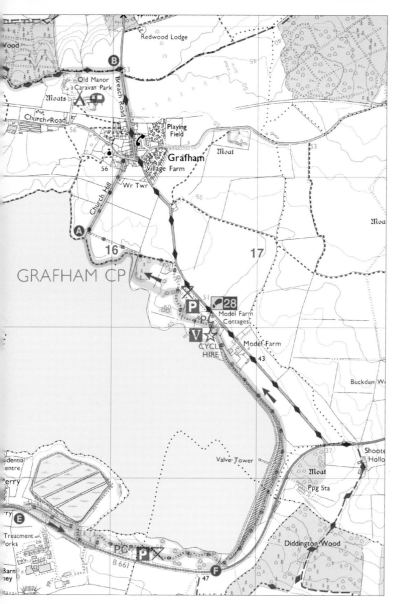

Rising once more, the way continues beside open farmland, later bearing left to enter Littless Wood. It is the most ancient woodland within the reserve and several nature trails wander off the main path. Leaving the trees behind, the track once more climbs across open farmland, the relative height allowing a fine view across the reservoir. Dropping alongside another area of reserve, the way shortly leads past the Fishing Lodge car park to the road outside Perry **D**.

Turn left through the village, the cycle track resuming again at the far end, just before the speed de-restriction sign **E**. Winding off into trees on the left, it meanders between the lake and road, before long passing behind another parking area. Keep going to the southern end of the dam **F**, where the path drops below the embankment. After a final climb to the service road at the far end cut behind the café back to the car park.

Further Information

The National Trust

Anyone who likes visiting places of natural beauty and/or historic interest has cause to be grateful to the National Trust. Without it, many such places would probably have vanished by now.

It was in response to the pressures on the countryside posed by the relentless march of Victorian industrialisation that the trust was set up in 1895. Its founders, inspired by the common goals of protecting and conserving Britain's national heritage and widening public access to it, were Sir Robert Hunter, Octavia Hill and Canon Rawnsley: respectively a solicitor, a social reformer and a clergyman. The latter was particularly influential. As a canon of Carlisle Cathedral and vicar of Crosthwaite (near Keswick), he was concerned about threats to the Lake District and had already been active in protecting footpaths and promoting public access to open countryside. After the flooding of Thirlmere in 1879 to create a large reservoir, he became increasingly convinced that the only effective way to guarantee protection was outright ownership of land.

The purpose of the National Trust is to preserve areas of natural beauty and sites of historic interest by acquisition, holding them in trust for the nation and making them available for public access and enjoyment. Some of its properties have been acquired through purchase, but many of the Trust's properties have been donated. Nowadays it is not only one of the biggest landowners in the country, but also one of the most active conservation charities, protecting 581,113 acres (253,176 ha) of land, including 555 miles (892km) of coastline, and over 300 historic properties in England, Wales and Northern Ireland. (There is a separate National Trust for Scotland, which was set up in 1931.)

Furthermore, once a piece of land has come under National Trust ownership, it is difficult for its status to be altered. As a result of parliamentary legislation in 1907, the Trust was given the right to declare its property inalienable, so ensuring that in any subsequent dispute it can appeal directly to parliament.

As it works towards its dual aims of conserving areas of attractive countryside and encouraging greater public access (not easy to reconcile in this age of mass tourism), the Trust provides an excellent service for walkers by creating new concessionary paths and waymarked trails, maintaining stiles and foot bridges and combating the ever-increasing problem of footpath erosion.

For details of membership, contact the National Trust at the address on page 95.

The Ramblers' Association

No organisation works more actively to protect and extend the rights and interests of walkers in the countryside than the Ramblers' Association. Its aims are clear: to foster a greater knowledge, love and care of the countryside; to assist in the protection and enhancement of public rights of way and areas of natural beauty; to work for greater public access to the countryside; and to encourage more people to take up rambling as a healthy, recreational leisure activity.

It was founded in 1935 when, following the setting up of a National Council of Ramblers' Federations in 1931, a number of federations earlier formed in London, Manchester, the Midlands and elsewhere came together to create a more effective pressure group, to deal with such problems as the disappearance and obstruction of footpaths, the prevention of access to open mountain and moorland and increasing hostility from landowners. This was the era of the mass trespasses, when there were sometimes violent

On Devil's Dyke, near Reach

confrontations between ramblers and gamekeepers, especially on the moorlands of the Peak District.

Since then the Ramblers' Association has played an influential role in preserving and developing the national footpath network, supporting the creation of national parks and encouraging the designation and waymarking of long-distance routes.

Our freedom to walk in the countryside is precarious and requires constant vigilance. As well as the perennial problems of footpaths being illegally obstructed, disappearing through lack of use or extinguished by housing or road construction, new dangers can spring up at any time.

It is to meet such problems and dangers that the Ramblers' Association exists and represents the interests of all walkers. The address to write to for information on the Ramblers' Association and how to become a member is given on page 95.

Walkers and the Law

The average walker in a national park or other popular walking area, armed with the appropriate Ordnance Survey map,

reinforced perhaps by a guidebook giving detailed walking instructions, is unlikely to run into legal difficulties, but it is useful to know something about the law relating to public rights of way. The right to walk over certain parts of the countryside has developed over a long period, and how such rights came into being is a complex subject, too lengthy to be discussed here. The following comments are intended simply as a helpful guide, backed up by the Countryside Access Charter, a concise summary of walkers' rights and obligations drawn up by the Countryside Agency (see page 94).

Basically there are two main kinds of public rights of way: footpaths (for walkers only) and bridleways (for walkers, riders on horseback and pedal cyclists). Footpaths and bridleways are shown by broken green lines on Ordnance Survey Explorer maps and broken red lines on Landranger maps. There is also a third category, called byways: chiefly broad tracks (green lanes) or farm roads, which walkers, riders and cyclists have to share, usually only occasionally, with motor vehicles. Many of these public paths have been in existence for hundreds of years and some even originated as prehistoric trackways

Countryside Access Charter

Your rights of way are:

- public footpaths – on foot only. Sometimes waymarked in yellow
- bridleways – on foot, horseback and pedal cycle. Sometimes waymarked in blue
- byways (usually old roads), most 'roads used as public paths' and, of course, public roads – all traffic has the right of way

Use maps, signs and waymarks to check rights of way. Ordnance Survey Explorer and Landranger maps show most public rights of way

On rights of way you can:

- take a pram, pushchair or wheelchair if practicable
- take a dog (on a lead or under close control)
- take a short route round an illegal obstruction or remove it sufficiently to get past

You have a right to go for recreation to:

- public parks and open spaces – on foot
- most commons near older towns and cities – on foot and sometimes on horseback
- private land where the owner has a formal agreement with the local authority

In addition you can use the following by local or established custom or consent, but ask for advice if you are unsure:

- many areas of open country, such as moorland, fell and coastal areas, especially those in the care of the National Trust, and some commons
- some woods and forests, especially those owned by the Forestry Commission
- country parks and picnic sites
- most beaches
- canal towpaths
- some private paths and tracks Consent sometimes extends to horse-riding and cycling

For your information:

- county councils and London boroughs maintain and record rights of way, and register commons
- obstructions, dangerous animals, harassment and misleading signs on rights of way are illegal and you should report them to the county council
- paths across fields can be ploughed, but must normally be reinstated within two weeks
- landowners can require you to leave land to which you have no right of access
- motor vehicles are normally permitted only on roads, byways and some 'roads used as public paths'

and have been in constant use for well over 2,000 years. Ways known as RUPPs (roads used as public paths) still appear on some maps. The legal definition of such byways is ambiguous and they are gradually being reclassified as footpaths, bridleways or byways.

The term 'right of way' means exactly what it says. It gives right of passage over what, in the vast majority of cases, is private land, and you are required to keep to the line of the path and not stray on to the land on either side. If you inadvertently wander off the right of way – either because of faulty map-reading or because the route is not clearly indicated on the ground – you are technically trespassing and the wisest course is to ask the nearest

available person (farmer or fellow walker) to direct you back to the correct route. There are stories about unpleasant confrontations between walkers and farmers at times, but in general most farmers are co-operative when responding to a genuine and polite request for assistance in route-finding.

Obstructions can sometimes be a problem and probably the most common of these is where a path across a field has been ploughed up. It is legal for a farmer to plough up a path provided that he restores it within two weeks, barring exceptionally bad weather. This does not always happen and here the walker is presented with a dilemma: to follow the line of the path, even if this inevitably means treading on crops, or to walk around the edge of the field. The latter course of action often seems the best but this means that you would be trespassing and not keeping to the exact line of the path. In the case of other obstructions which may block a path (illegal fences and locked gates etc), common sense has to be used in order to negotiate them by the easiest method – detour or removal. You should only ever remove as much as is necessary to get through, and if you can easily go round the obstruction without causing any damage, then you should do so. If you have any problems negotiating rights of way, you should report the matter to the rights of way department of the relevant council, which will take action with the landowner concerned.

Apart from rights of way enshrined by law, there are a number of other paths available to walkers. Permissive or concessionary paths have been created where a landowner has given permission for the public to use a particular route across his land. The main problem with these is that, as they have been granted as a concession, there is no legal right to use them and therefore they can be extinguished at any time. In practice, many of these concessionary routes have been established on and owned either by large public bodies such as the Forestry Commission, or by a private one, such as the National Trust, and as these mainly encourage walkers to use their paths, they are unlikely to be closed unless a change of ownership occurs.

Walkers also have free access to country parks except where requested to keep away from certain areas for ecological reasons, e.g wildlife protection, woodland regeneration, etc), canal towpaths and most beaches. By custom, though not by right, you are generally free to walk across the open and uncultivated higher land of mountain, moorland and fell, but this varies from area to area and from one season to another – grouse moors, for example, will be out of bounds during the breeding and shooting seasons and some open areas are used as Ministry of Defence firing ranges, for which reason access will be restricted. In some areas the situation has been clarified as a result of 'access agreements' between the landowners and either the county council or the national park authority, which clearly define when and where you can walk over such open country.

 ## Walking Safety

Although the reasonably gentle countryside that is the subject of this book offers no real dangers to walkers at any time of the year, it is still advisable to take sensible precautions and follow certain well-tried guidelines.

Always take with you both warm and waterproof clothing and sufficient food and drink. Wear suitable footwear such as strong walking boots or shoes that give a good grip over stony ground, on slippery

The gatehouse of Ramsey Abbey

Grantchester Meadows

walking conditions, with firm ground underfoot and a clarity unique to this time of the year. The most difficult hazard likely to be encountered is mud, especially when walking along woodland and field paths, farm tracks and bridleways – the latter in particular can often get churned up by cyclists and horses. In summer, an additional difficulty may be narrow and overgrown paths, particularly along the edges of cultivated fields. Neither should constitute a major problem provided that the appropriate footwear is worn.

slopes and in muddy conditions. Try to obtain a local weather forecast and bear it in mind before you start. Do not be afraid to abandon your proposed route and return to your starting point in the event of a sudden and unexpected deterioration in the weather.

All the walks described in this book will be safe to do, given due care and respect, even during the winter. Indeed, a crisp, fine winter day often provides perfect

 Useful Organisations

Cambridgeshire County Council
Environment Division,
Shire Hall, Castle Hill,
Cambridge CB3 0AP
Tel. 01223 717445

Campaign to Protect Rural England
128 Southwark Street,
London SE1 0SW
Tel. 020 7981 2800

The village of Lode in spring

Camping and Caravanning Club
Greenfields House, Westwood Way,
Coventry CV4 8BR
Tel. 0204 7647 6809
www.campingandcaravanningclub.co.uk

Countryside Agency
John Dower House, Crescent Place,
Cheltenham, Gloucestershire GL50 3RA
Tel. 01242 521381

Forestry Commission
Silvan House, 231 Corstorphine Road,
Edinburgh EH12 7AT Tel. 0131 334 0303

Long Distance Walkers' Association
Bank House, High Street, Wrotham,
Sevenoaks, Kent TN15 7AE
Tel. 01732 883705

National Trust
Membership and general enquiries:
PO Box 39, Warrington
WA5 7WD
Tel. 0870 458 4000
East Anglia Regional Office:
Westley Bottom, Bury St Edmunds,
Suffolk IP33 3WD
Tel. 01284 747500

Ordnance Survey
Romsey Road, Maybush,
Southampton SO16 4GU
Tel. 08456 05 05 05 (Lo-call)

Ramblers' Association
2nd Floor, Camelford House,
87–90 Albert Embankment,
London SE1 7TW
Tel. 020 7339 8500

Tourist information:
East of England Tourist Board
Toppesfield Hall, Hadleigh,
Suffolk IP7 7DN
Tel. 01473 822922
Local tourist information centres:
Cambridge: 01223 457574
Ely: 01353 662062
Huntingdon: 01480 388588
Peterborough: 01733 452336
Wisbech: 01945 583263

Peterborough City Council
Town Hall,
Bridge Street,
Peterborough PE1 1QT
Tel. 01733 747474

Youth Hostels Association
Trevelyan House,
Dimple Road, Matlock,
Derbyshire DE4 3YH
Tel. 01629 592600

Ordnance Survey maps of Cambridgeshire and the Fens

The area of Cambridgeshire is covered by
Ordnance Survey 1:50 000 (1¼ inches to
1 mile or 2cm to 1km) scale Landranger
map sheets 142, 143, 153, 154. These all-
purpose maps are packed with information
to help you explore the area. Viewpoints,
picnic sites, places of interest and caravan
and camping sites are shown, as well as
public rights of way information such as
footpaths and bridleways.

To examine the area in more detail and
especially if you are planning walks,
Explorer maps at 1:25 000 (2½ inches to
1 mile or 4cm to 1km) scale are ideal:

208 Bedford and St Neots
209 Cambridge
210 Newmarket & Haverhill
225 Huntingdon & St Ives
226 Ely & Newmarket
227 Peterborough
228 March & Ely
235 Wisbech & Peterborough North
236 King's Lynn, Downham Market &
      Swaffham

To get to the Cambridgeshire area use the
Ordnance Survey OS Travel Map-Route
Great Britain at 1:625 000 (1 inch to 10
miles or 4cm to 25km) scale or Ordnance
Survey OS Travel Map-Road 5 (East
Midlands and East Anglia including
London) or 8 (South East England includ-
ing London) at 1:250 000 (1 inch to 4
miles or 1cm to 2.5km) scale. Ordnance
Survey maps and guides are available
from most booksellers, stationers and
newsagents

Further Information

www.totalwalking.co.uk

www.totalwalking.co.uk
is the official website of the Jarrold
Pathfinder and Short Walks guides. This
interactive website features a wealth of
information for walkers – from the latest
news on route diversions and advice from
professional walkers to product news, free
sample walks and promotional offers.

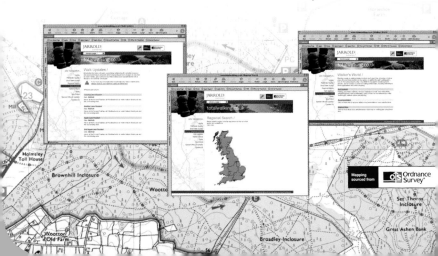